Paper Toys That Fly, Soar, Zoom & Whistle

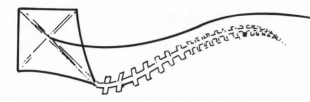

Paper Toys That Fly, Soar, Zoom & Whistle

E. Richard Churchill

Illustrated by James Michaels

Sterling Publishing Co., Inc.   New York

For Chum—who is not only my wife but who is also my best friend—with love.

J
745.54
C4759

With special thanks to the students of Brentwood Middle School, Greeley, Colorado, and to the engineering students of Colorado State University, Fort Collins, Colorado, who provided designs and suggestions which were, and are, much appreciated.

Edited by Timothy Nolan.

Library of Congress Cataloging-in-Publication Data

Churchill, E. Richard (Elmer Richard)
    Paper toys that fly, soar, zoom, and whistle / by E. Richard
Churchill ; illustrated by James Michaels.
        p.   cm.
    Includes index.
    ISBN 0-8069-6840-0
    1. Paper toy making.   I. Title.
TT174.5.P3C48   1989
688.7'28—dc19   88-30311
                                                                 CIP

    1   3   5   7   9   10   8   6   4   2

Copyright © 1989 by E. Richard Churchill
Published by Sterling Publishing Co., Inc.
Two Park Avenue, New York, N.Y. 10016
Distributed in Canada by Oak Tree Press Ltd.
% Canadian Manda Group, P.O. Box 920, Station U
Toronto, Ontario, Canada M8Z 5P9
Distributed in Great Britain and Europe by Cassell PLC
Artillery House, Artillery Row, London SW1P 1RT, England
Distributed in Australia by Capricorn Ltd.
P.O. Box 665, Lane Cove, NSW 2066
Manufactured in the United States of America
All rights reserved
Sterling ISBN 0-8069-6840-0 Trade

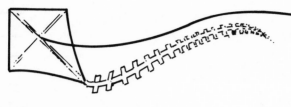

Contents

METRIC EQUIVALENCY CHART

MM—MILLIMETRES   CM—CENTIMETRES

INCHES TO MILLIMETRES AND CENTIMETRES

INCHES	MM	CM	INCHES	CM	INCHES	CM
⅛	3	0.3	9	22.9	30	76.2
¼	6	0.6	10	25.4	31	78.7
⅜	10	1.0	11	27.9	32	81.3
½	13	1.3	12	30.5	33	83.8
⅝	16	1.6	13	33.0	34	86.4
¾	19	1.9	14	35.6	35	88.9
⅞	22	2.2	15	38.1	36	91.4
1	25	2.5	16	40.6	37	94.0
1¼	32	3.2	17	43.2	38	96.5
1½	38	3.8	18	45.7	39	99.1
1¾	44	4.4	19	48.3	40	101.6
2	51	5.1	20	50.8	41	104.1
2½	64	6.4	21	53.3	42	106.7
3	76	7.6	22	55.9	43	109.2
3½	89	8.9	23	58.4	44	111.8
4	102	10.2	24	61.0	45	114.3
4½	114	11.4	25	63.5	46	116.8
5	127	12.7	26	66.0	47	119.4
6	152	15.2	27	68.6	48	121.9
7	178	17.8	28	71.1	49	124.5
8	203	20.3	29	73.7	50	127.0

YARDS TO METRES

YARDS	METRES	YARDS	METRES	YARDS	METRES	YARDS	METRES	YARDS	METRES
⅛	0.11	2⅛	1.94	4⅛	3.77	6⅛	5.60	8⅛	7.43
¼	0.23	2¼	2.06	4¼	3.89	6¼	5.72	8¼	7.54
⅜	0.34	2⅜	2.17	4⅜	4.00	6⅜	5.83	8⅜	7.66
½	0.46	2½	2.29	4½	4.11	6½	5.94	8½	7.77
⅝	0.57	2⅝	2.40	4⅝	4.23	6⅝	6.06	8⅝	7.89
¾	0.69	2¾	2.51	4¾	4.34	6¾	6.17	8¾	8.00
⅞	0.80	2⅞	2.63	4⅞	4.46	6⅞	6.29	8⅞	8.12
1	0.91	3	2.74	5	4.57	7	6.40	9	8.23
1⅛	1.03	3⅛	2.86	5⅛	4.69	7⅛	6.52	9⅛	8.34
1¼	1.14	3¼	2.97	5¼	4.80	7¼	6.63	9¼	8.46
1⅜	1.26	3⅜	3.09	5⅜	4.91	7⅜	6.74	9⅜	8.57
1½	1.37	3½	3.20	5½	5.03	7½	6.86	9½	8.69
1⅝	1.49	3⅝	3.31	5⅝	5.14	7⅝	6.97	9⅝	8.80
1¾	1.60	3¾	3.43	5¾	5.26	7¾	7.09	9¾	8.92
1⅞	1.71	3⅞	3.54	5⅞	5.37	7⅞	7.20	9⅞	9.03
2	1.83	4	3.66	6	5.49	8	7.32	10	9.14

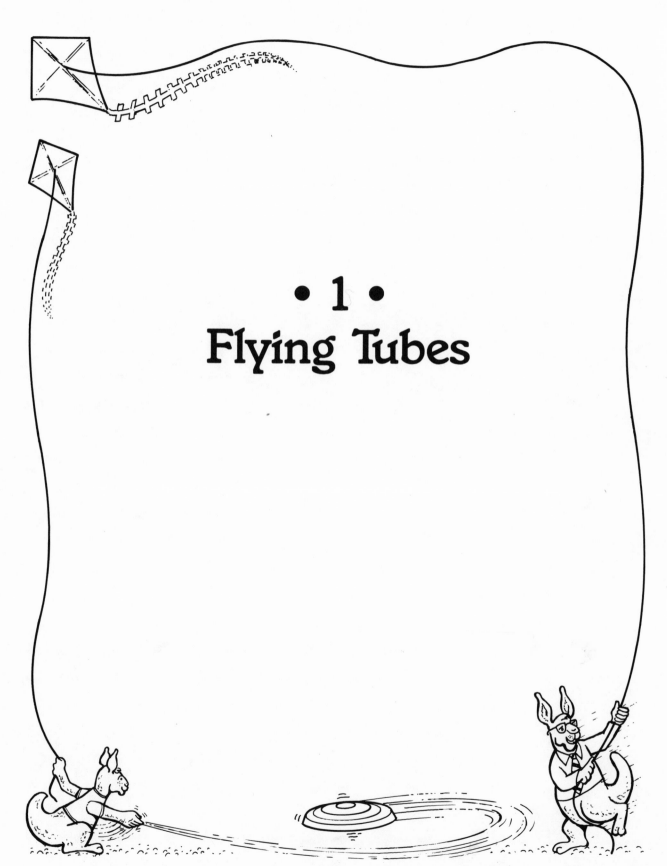

• 1 •
Flying Tubes

When we think of flying paper toys, we usually think of airplanes, but there are a number of other flying paper toys, such as hollow tubes. These take only a few seconds to make, are lots of fun to fly, and often fly surprisingly fast and far.

Short and Fast

To build Short and Fast you need a sheet of notebook paper and three paper clips.

Begin by folding the paper double as shown in Illus. 1. The dotted line shows your next fold.

Illus. 1

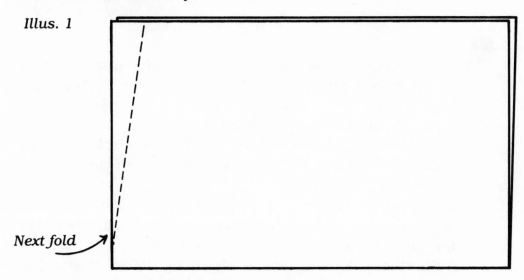

Next fold

Now make the fold in Illus. 2. It starts about one inch in back of the first fold you made.

Illus. 2

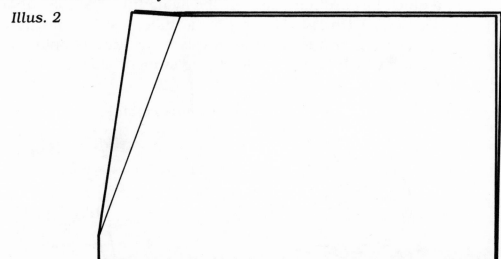

Now begin rolling the paper into a tube or cylinder. Roll from the side opposite the fold you just made in the last step. Try to make the hollow tube about 1 inch across the open end. When you have it rolled, it should look like Illus. 3. Note that the fold you made before now stands up.

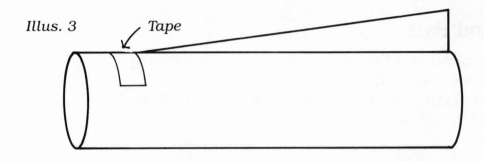

Illus. 3   Tape

It's a good idea to stick a little strip of transparent tape on the side of Short and Fast as seen in Illus. 3. The paper clips will keep the tube from unrolling, but the tape does make it a little easier to handle.

The folded edges that stand up from the tube act as a stabilizer. A stabilizer just keeps flying toys flying straight and evenly.

Now slip the three paper clips over the nose of Short and Fast, and space them evenly around the open nose. (The nose is the end away from the stabilizer.)

Short and Fast is now ready to fly. To get it going or launch it, cup your hand and hold the tube loosely, straight down at your side. Now, lift your hand and arm in a quick forward move and let the flying tube just roll out of your cupped hand. This gives the tube or cylinder a little spin as it starts forward. It is this same kind of spinning motion which keeps a bullet flying straight after it leaves a rifle barrel.

It does spin like a bullet!

Practise launching Short and Fast with this underhand motion until you can release it smoothly. (Most of the flying tubes are launched this way).

If Short and Fast stalls or wobbles in the air, you may need to add another paper clip.

When you have this tube flying well, try a little change. Make another Short and Fast but roll it more tightly, so that it is only about ½ inch across the open end. See what difference this makes in its flight.

Whiner

Begin your Whiner by folding a sheet of notebook paper double so that it looks like Illus. 4. About midway along the folded edge make a cut ½ inch or so long.

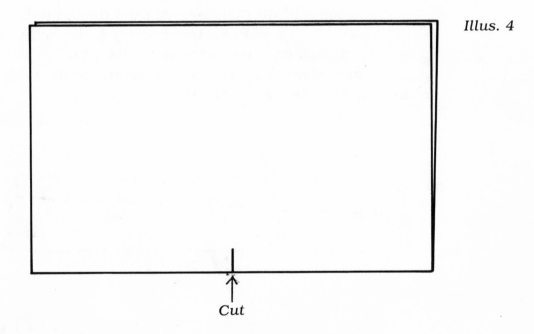

Illus. 4

Cut

Roll the paper into a cylinder, beginning with the side opposite the cut. Make the roll about ½ inch across the open end.

Now turn the cylinder into a cone by making one end smaller than the other. Hold one end of the rolled paper so that it stays about ½ inch across the opening, and loosen the other end so that it gets wider. If the paper isn't very stiff you may need to coax it a bit.

When the larger end is about 1 inch across, take two pieces of transparent tape and look at Illus. 5 to see where to place them. About ¼ inch in front of the cut is just right. If your Whiner tries to unroll, put another little strip of tape just in back of the nose.

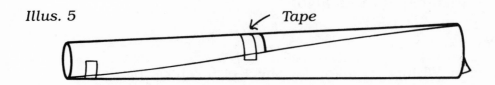

Illus. 5   Tape

Now fold the stabilizer up from the cut to the larger open end of your Whiner. Don't worry if the stabilizer is just a little higher at the rear than at its front; it's supposed to be that way. Your Whiner is about ready to launch, and should look like Illus. 6.

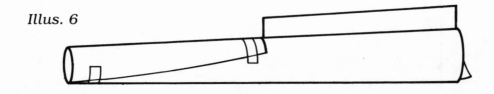

Illus. 6

Slip two or three paper clips onto the nose of your Whiner, and launch it almost as you would a dart. Hold it with your index finger on the tail; then launch it with a quick snap of your wrist.

If Whiner slows down in the middle of its flight, just add another paper clip or two. Your Whiner should surprise you by how far it flies.

When you fly the Whiner indoors and everything is very still you should hear a faint whining sound from the vibration of its stabilizer. Don't worry if you can't hear it. Some Whiners don't whine very loudly.

Remember whenever you fly any of your paper toys to be careful! With the weight of the paper clips on their noses some of them really get out and move. You may think they can't break a window, but why take chances? They *can* knock over little china figures and delicate things of that sort, so look before you fly.

Three in One

Begin your Three in One by cutting a piece of notebook paper about 5 inches wide. Cut a second strip of paper 1 inch wide; then cut one more strip 1 × 5 inches.

Begin rolling the large piece of paper into a hollow tube, with the long side next to you. Form the tube about ½ inch across the open end. Naturally, the cylinder or tube will be 11½ inches long.

Use three pieces of transparent tape to hold the tube together so that it looks like Illus. 7; then lay the tube aside for a few minutes. Form each of the narrow strips of paper into a loop, and use a piece of tape to hold the loop together. The finished loops should look like Illus. 8, except that one will be much larger than the other one.

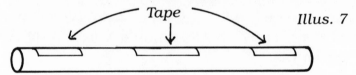

Tape *Illus. 7*

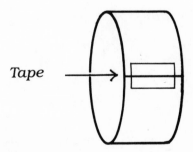

Illus. 8

Tape →

Let's put Three in One together. Tape one of the loops onto the top of one end of the tube (either loop on either end is fine).

Place the loop on top of the tube. Pull off a strip of tape about 2½ inches long. Slip the tape through the inside of the loop and press it down so that about ¾ inch of tape sticks out on either side, as in Illus. 9.

Place the loop on top of one end of the tube so that the front edge of the loop and the end of the tube are even. Press down the end of the tape which extends over the main part of the tube.

Illus. 9

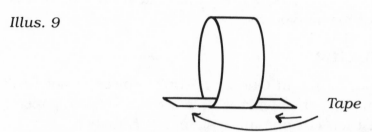

Tape

Push the other end of the tape into the hollow center of the tube. Use your finger to make sure it sticks tightly to the inside of the tube. Illus. 10 shows Three in One at this stage.

Illus. 10

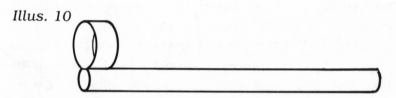

Now repeat this process with the other loop. When this step is finished your Three in One should look like Illus. 11. It is ready to launch.

Illus. 11

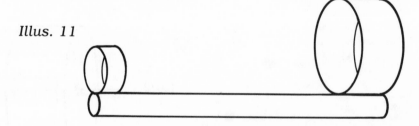

Hold it near the middle of the main tube and launch it gently. Three in One will fly in a nice gliding path if it's not thrown hard. Launch it with the small loop in front. If you want to know why, just try launching it with the large loop in front.

14

After you have flown this surprising tube a few times, try some experiments. Don't be satisfied with just one way of making any paper toy. Always feel free to try some other ideas and see how they work. Remember, the worst that can happen is that a new idea won't work, but sometimes it works better than the original.

Make a Three in One with the loops so that the main tube is inside the loops. See how this changes the way it performs.

Try making a model with the loops 1½ inches wide instead of 1 inch wide; then make one with loops only ½ inch wide. Consider making the loops smaller or even larger.

Try slipping a paper clip into the nose of a model if it stalls or seems unable to glide properly. This should not be necessary on most models, but when you make big changes the paper clip may help.

Cylinder

The nice thing about the Cylinder is that it requires no tape, no clips, and no cutting. Just a few folds turn a sheet of notebook paper into a great flying tube.

Begin with the paper's short side closest to you. Fold the bottom edge up along the dotted line in Illus. 12. This fold should be ⅓ of the way up the paper. Crease the fold into place by running the top of your thumbnail along the fold.

Illus. 13 shows the paper after the first fold. The dotted line shows where to make your next fold.

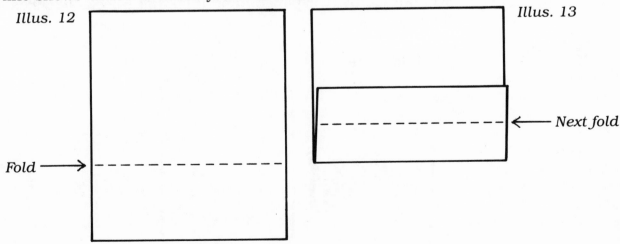

Illus. 12

Illus. 13

Fold ⟶

⟵ *Next fold*

Fold the bottom of the paper along this dotted line (just fold the bottom part of the paper in half). Crease the fold, and your Cylinder now looks like Illus. 14. At this point the paper is four layers thick along the folded area.

Illus. 14

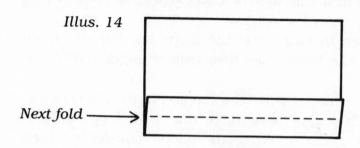

Next fold ⟶

The dotted line in Illus. 14 shows your final fold. Fold the bottom part of the paper in half and crease the fold, so that your Cylinder looks like Illus. 15. The folded part of the paper is beginning to get pretty thick with all those layers of paper, isn't it?

Illus. 15

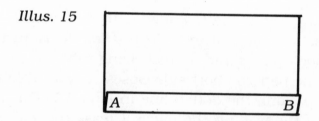

It is now time to form the Cylinder. Hold the paper at points A and B in Illus. 15. Bring these two points together without folding the paper. Bend it so that it looks like Illus. 16.

Illus. 16

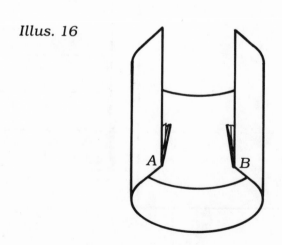

When the points come together, slip A into B. Do this by pushing point A between the thick layers of folded paper and the single layer of unfolded paper. Once the two sides of the Cylinder overlap, slide point A about 1½ inches into point B.

To finish your Cylinder, very carefully fold up the single layer of paper where point B overlaps to form a stabilizer. Fold the edge at an angle, so that the stabilizer begins right at point B and angles back. It should be about ½ inch wide at the tail of the Cylinder. The dotted line in Illus. 17 shows this fold.

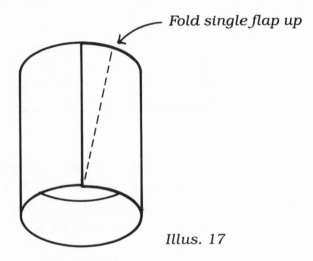

Fold single flap up

Illus. 17

Fold the stabilizer into place so that it sticks straight up, and your Cylinder is ready for launch.

To launch your flying Cylinder, hold it underhanded. Give your hand and arm a quick movement forward and upwards, and let the Cylinder roll out of your cupped fingers. Don't try to throw it too hard. Just give it a quick forward toss. Try launching it faster or slower until you discover just the proper launch speed. This flying tube is a real surprise because it flies so well.

Hollow Flier

The cardboard tube of a roll of toilet paper is just what you need for the main body of the Hollow Flier. If you don't have one handy you can make a tube from a file card, so don't unravel all the toilet paper. The tube needs to be about 4 inches long and about 1¾ inches across. It should be perfectly round. When you find or make this tube, put it aside for a few minutes.

Cut three pieces of paper, each 4 inches long and 2¼ inches wide. Notebook or typing paper is just fine for these three pieces.

Fold one of the pieces along the middle the long way so that it looks like Illus. 18. The dotted line shows where to make your next fold.

Illus. 18

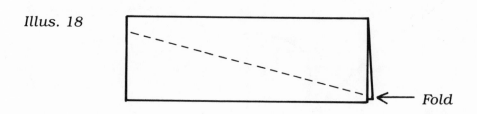

← *Fold*

Fold up the side nearer to you along the dotted line and crease the fold into place; then turn the paper over and fold the other side in exactly the same way. Now fold the other two pieces of paper in exactly the same way. These three pieces of paper will be the stabilizers for the Flier.

Now you'll need transparent tape or glue to attach the stabilizers. Either works just fine.

Hold one of the pieces of paper by its central fold and place the open side of the paper against the tube. When you do this the two flaps you folded will fit right onto the side of the tube. Tape or glue them onto the tube, so that your Flier looks like Illus. 19.

Illus. 19

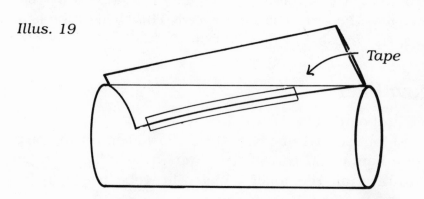

Tape

Now do the same with the other two stabilizers. Space them so that each stabilizer is one-third of the way around the tube from the other stabilizers. Once all three are in place your Flier is about ready to launch.

Just for the fun of it, try launching the Flier now. The nose of the Flier is the side at which the stabilizers are lower. Launch it underhand, like the other tubes.

The Flier's first launch is a little disappointing.

The reason it flutters and stalls is that it has no weight in the nose. For this, use paper clips. Clip three or four clips evenly around the tube on the Flier's nose. Now launch it again. It should fly a bit better now.

Adding weight is called adjusting the trim, or trimming. Pilots trim their airplanes by adjusting flaps and elevators. We trim our flying tubes by adding nose weight.

Keep testing the paper clips on your Flier. Just be sure to space the paper clips evenly around the nose.

When your Flier suddenly begins to fly faster, straighter, and farther than before, you've got the right number of clips. With a bit of experimenting you will get just the right amount of weight. Just remember not to launch it in the direction of windows, pictures, vases, china knickknacks, and the like.

The toilet paper did it!

Who broke the vase?

Flying Fins

Begin with a piece of notebook or typing paper. Cut a piece from it about 8½ × 2½ inches. One of the nice things about most flying paper toys is they do not have to be any exact size. If you happen to make a piece of paper a little larger or a little smaller than called for, the project usually works just fine.

While you have the scissors handy, cut out two more pieces of paper. Make both of them 1 inch wide and 5 inches long.

Now roll the large piece of paper, with the long side closest to you, into a hollow tube ¼ inch across. To hold the finished tube together, use two or three pieces of transparent tape, as in Illus. 20.

Illus. 20

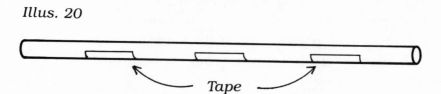

Tape

Illus. 21

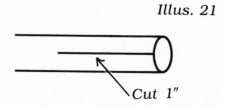

Cut 1"

Push one scissor point inside the hollow tube and very carefully cut straight down the tube for a 1-inch cut, as in Illus. 21.

Now make a second cut just like the first one, directly opposite the first cut.

Make a third cut halfway between the two cuts you just made, and a fourth cut opposite the third. Make both of them 1 inch long.

Now you have four cuts in one end of the tube. If all went well, they are evenly spaced, but if there is a little more space between two cuts than between two other cuts, don't worry.

Just for fun, try launching this tube just like a dart or with your index finger behind it. It just flutters almost helplessly in the air. This is because it has no stability.

Now fold each of the smaller pieces of paper in half. You should have double-thick papers 1 inch wide and 2½ inches long. That's right—these fins are going to stabilize the tube.

Slip one of these fins into any two cuts in the tube which are next to each other. Illus. 22 shows how.

Now slide the second fin into the other two cuts. Be sure each fin is centered so that the same amount of material sticks out on either side of the tube.

Now launch your tube again. It should fly in a pretty straight path. It will also cover a lot more distance than when you tried it without its stabilizing fins.

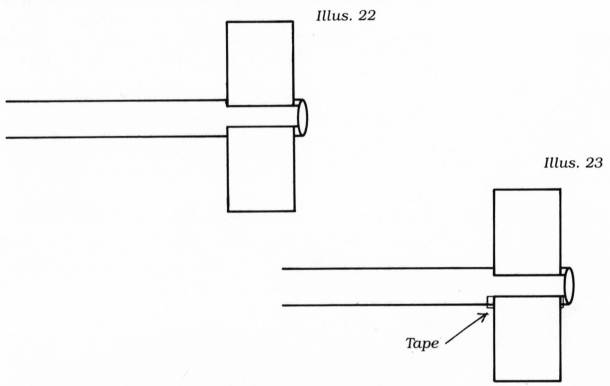

Illus. 22

Illus. 23

Tape

If you wish, use a piece of tape to fasten each fin into place so that it won't slip out during a hard landing. Run the tape along the end of the tube so that the tape overlaps one side of the fin, as in Illus. 23.

You might want to make the fins out of a file card. In that case cut each fin 1 inch wide and only 2½ inches long since you won't have to fold it double.

You may also want to use a plastic drinking straw for the tube, so that you won't have to roll the tube and tape it together.

Do some research into Flying Fins. Make a tube longer than 8½ inches; then try a model that is shorter. See what happens if you make the fins longer or shorter, wider or narrower than in the original Flying Fin.

Cone

A flying Cone takes about ten seconds to make and flies amazingly well. Just take a sheet of notebook paper and start rolling it loosely along the long side.

As you roll it, begin making one end, the nose-to-be, tighter and let the other end loosen. This forms a sort of spiral as you turn the paper into a cone.

Roll the Cone so that it is about ¼ inch across the nose and 1¾ inches across the tail. Don't worry about the point of paper extending out from the tail. Your Cone should look like Illus. 24. Look at this illustration to see where to tape the Cone.

Slip one or two paper clips onto the Cone's nose and launch it with an underhand swing.

Illus. 24

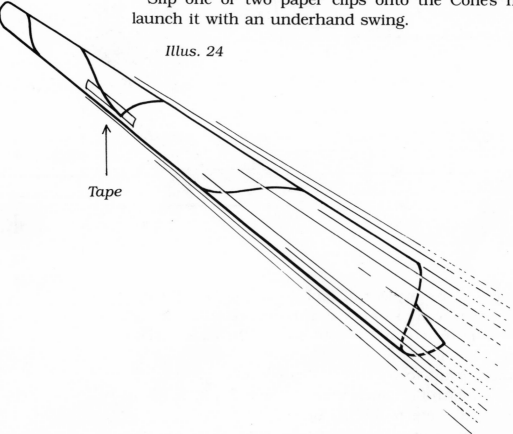

Tape

The Cone does a nice job of flying and is so easy to make you may want to spend your whole day flying it, but keep something in mind—most teachers and parents don't appreciate having Cones fly through their classrooms and bedrooms!

Whistler

The Whistler is another flying cone, but it's made from a 4 × 6-inch file card.

Roll the card the long way into a cone, about ¼ inch across the nose and 1¼ inches across the tail.

Hold the rolled cone in place with a piece of tape as in Illus. 25. Note the little V where the edges of the card do not quite overlap at the tail. When you have this V, your Whistler is exactly the right size.

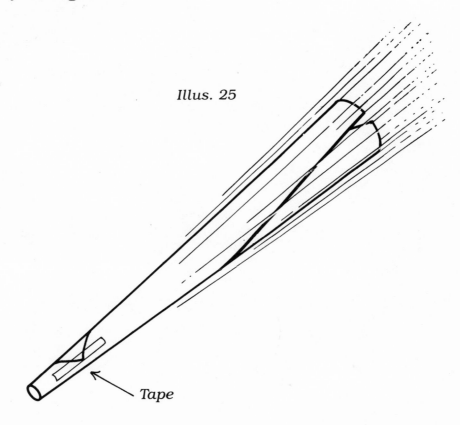

Illus. 25

Tape

Slip two paper clips onto the nose of the Whistler and launch it with a quick underhand snap of your hand and arm. Give the Whistler a little bit of sideways roll as it slips off the tips of your fingers.

Be prepared for a fast, long flight. Whistler takes off like a bullet and really goes. To anyone who has not seen flying tubes and cones, Whistler will come as a total surprise.

• 2 •
Flying Discs

You don't need to buy a flying disc to have one. You can make many different kinds by using common paper plates. Any kind of paper plate will do, whether it be the plain white ones, the plastic-coated plates, or the ones made of plastic foam. Keep in mind, though, that if the directions say to use five paper plates, you'll need fewer if you're using the heavier ones. But, as with all our other projects, don't be afraid to experiment.

Don't use the family supply of paper plates for your flying discs just before a picnic or cookout!

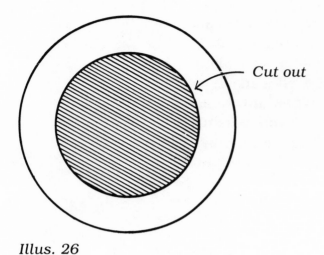

Illus. 26

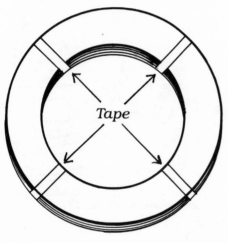

Illus. 27

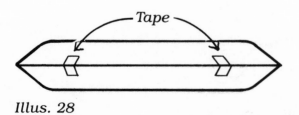

Illus. 28

Super Sailer

For this disc you need five or six paper plates. You also need scissors and tape. Masking tape is the best for this, but transparent tape works well, too.

Begin by cutting the centers out of all the paper plates except one. Carefully poke the point of the scissors through the middle of the plate (don't poke your finger, trying to poke the plate!) and cut where the rim of the plate meets the bottom. Your Sailer should look like Illus. 26.

Save the pieces you cut out of the plates, because you may need them for other projects.

Stack the plate rims together as in Illus. 27; then use about 8 inches of tape to wrap around the stack of plates. Hold the paper plates together tightly as you wrap the tape, so that they won't slip apart in flight.

Wrap the tape around the plates three more times, each time a quarter of the way around the ring. Put the plate rims down, with the side you eat off facing up.

Now take the paper plate you did not cut and put it upside down over the rims. Tape the top onto the plate rims with six or seven short pieces of tape. Space them evenly and press them firmly into place. Your Super Sailer should look like Illus. 28. If it does, it is ready for launch.

To launch this or any flying disc, use a backhand motion. Hold the disc with your thumb on top and the rest of your hand curled around underneath. Point it towards your body. To launch it, just snap your hand and wrist back, and away it should sail. Illus. 29 shows this launch.

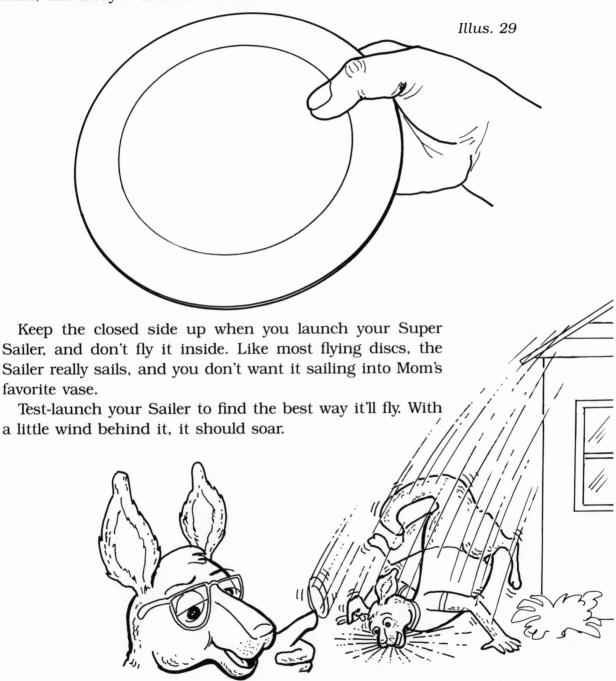

Illus. 29

Keep the closed side up when you launch your Super Sailer, and don't fly it inside. Like most flying discs, the Sailer really sails, and you don't want it sailing into Mom's favorite vase.

Test-launch your Sailer to find the best way it'll fly. With a little wind behind it, it should soar.

Remember one thing—it's a lot easier to make a new Super Sailer than it is to fall off the roof getting the old one!

Crown

Begin this disc by placing two or three paper plates together, face up. Use five or six 3-inch strips of tape to fasten the plates together. Space the tape strips evenly around the rims of the plates and be sure to press them firmly into place. Again, masking tape is great but transparent tape works well, also. Look at Illus. 30 to see where to place the tape. Now set this part of your Crown aside for a moment.

Illus. 30

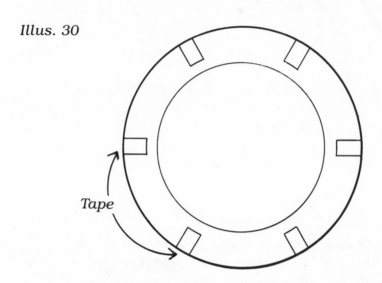

Tape

Take another paper plate and, very carefully, push the point of your scissors through it right where the bottom of the plate meets the rim; then cut straight across the middle of the paper plate until you reach the other side or the plate's bottom. Illus. 31 shows this cut.

Don't poke your finger with the point!

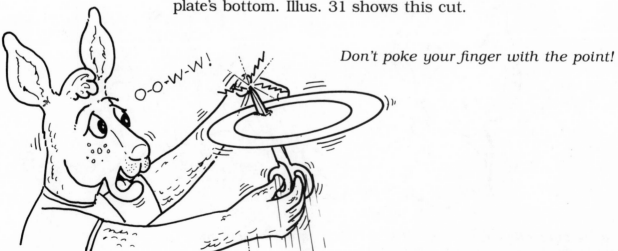

O-O-W-W!

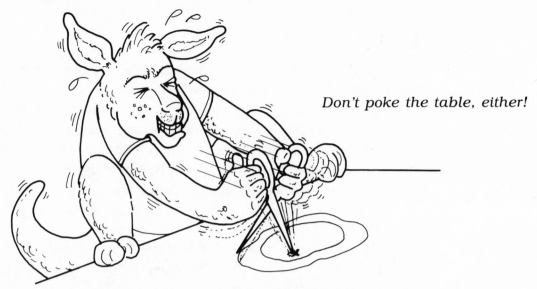

Don't poke the table, either!

The dotted lines in Illus. 31 show the next three cuts. These will divide the plate into eight equal parts.

Bend each point straight up, so that your Crown looks like Illus. 32 (now you can see why this disc is called the Crown).

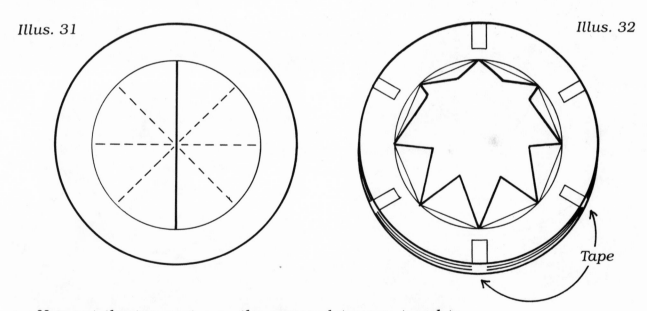

Illus. 31

Illus. 32

Tape

Now set the top part over the paper plates you taped together. Use about six strips of tape to attach the two parts. Try to space them evenly around the rim.

Your Crown is ready for its first test flight. You will probably find the Crown does not fly well into the wind but does a nice job with little or no breeze behind it. Use your backhand delivery and experiment.

UFO

Now you'll need two of the middle pieces from your Super Sailer.

UFO needs two or three paper plates, a sheet of notebook paper and a rubber band. A stapler will also be a big help.

Cut a 3-inch circle out of each paper plate, as neatly as you can. It's easier to draw the circle before you begin cutting, and to only cut one paper plate at a time. Illus. 33 shows this central cut. Cut out and throw away the darkened area.

When the paper plates have their centers cut out, use five or six short strips of tape to fasten them together. Illus. 34 shows where to place the tape.

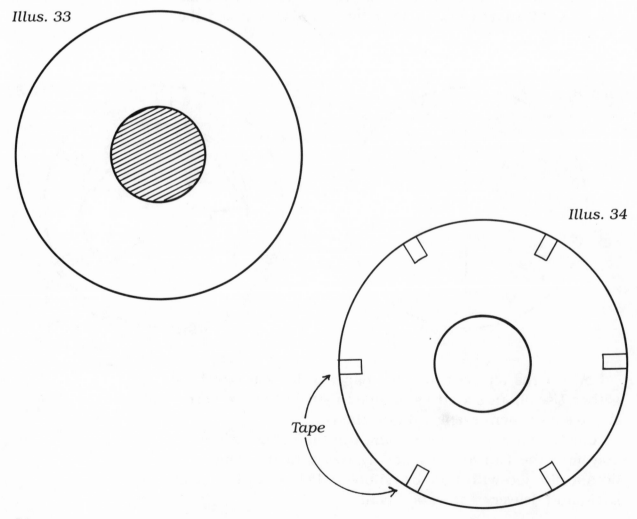

Illus. 33

Illus. 34

Tape

Now you need the central pieces from Super Sailer. Make a cut from the outer edge right to the middle of each circle; then make an identical cut about 1½ inches away. Illus. 35 shows these cuts. Remove the little triangle of material between the cuts and throw it away. Cut the little circle out of the middle that you see in Illus. 36. This little circle should be about ¼ inch across, though it wouldn't hurt if it were a little larger.

Now is the time for your stapler. If you don't have a stapler, tape will do the job just fine.

Illus. 35   *Illus. 36*

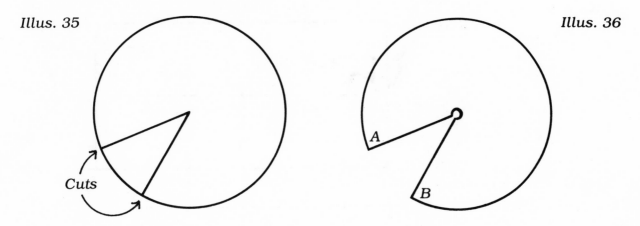

Look at Illus. 36. Pull edge A over so that it overlaps edge B about ½ inch. This should form the cone in Illus. 37, which also shows where to staple or tape the edges together. Form both of the round pieces into cones in this manner; then set one inside the other so that you have a double-thick cone.

Illus. 37

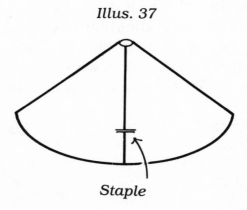

Staple

Now for the notebook paper. Cut a strip about 5 inches long and 1 inch wide. Start at one end and roll it into a tight tube about 1 inch long and ¼ inch across. Fasten the loose edge with a little bit of tape.

Fold the rest of the sheet of paper in half the long way. The dotted line in Illus. 38 shows this fold. This gives you a double sheet of paper about 4 inches wide. Roll it into a tight tube that will end up being about 4 inches long and ⅜ inch or so across. Fasten the loose edge with a strip of tape. Both these tubes are in Illus. 39.

Illus. 38

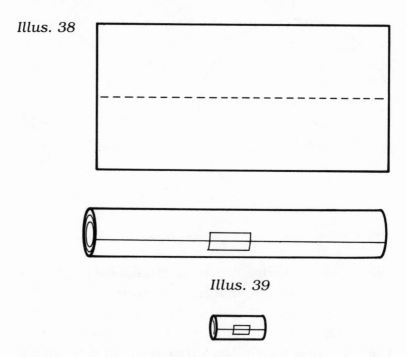

Illus. 39

Now you can assemble UFO. Take the rubber band and double it up; then slip the 1-inch rolled tube through the ends of the rubber band as shown in Illus. 40.

Push the rest of the rubber band through the hole in the top of the cones, as in Illus. 41. When the rubber band is through the hole, pull down on it hard to hold it in place so that the little paper tube won't slip away.

Illus. 40

Illus. 41

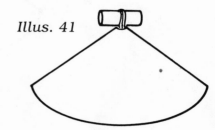

Now get the paper plates. Here comes the tricky part. What you have to do is pull the rubber band through the middle of the paper plates and slip the other paper tube (the longer one) through it. This will hold the disc together.

Take the cones and the short paper roll in one hand and turn them upside down, so that the open sides face upwards. Put the paper plates on top of the open cones, reach through the hole, and get a firm grip on the rubber band. Pull it through the hole so that it stretches a bit. Slip the longer rolled tube through the ends of the rubber band, and that's all there is to it.

When you're done, the ends of the long tube should rest on either side of the hole, and the whole thing should look like Illus. 42. (Don't be afraid to ask for help—sometimes a third hand is needed!)

It is a good idea to put a couple of strips of tape along the edges of the cone so that it does not slip around when UFO makes a hard landing. Illus. 43 shows where to put them.

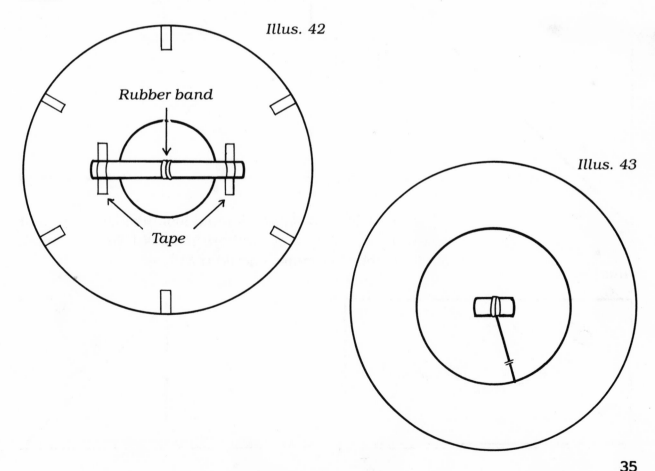

Illus. 42

Rubber band

Tape

Illus. 43

Pentadisc

For this disc you can put away the paper plates. Five sheets of notebook paper and some tape will get you into business with this project.

Begin by making squares out of the notebook paper. To turn a rectangle into a square fold one corner over, as in Illus. 44, and just cut off the dark part of the paper. Unfold the paper and you have a square. This is a good thing to remember.

Now fold your square along the dotted line as shown in Illus. 45.

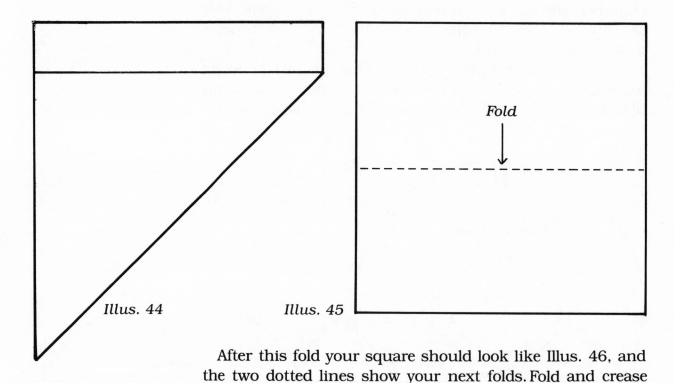

Illus. 44

Illus. 45

After this fold your square should look like Illus. 46, and the two dotted lines show your next folds. Fold and crease them well. Your Pentadisc should now look like Illus. 47.

Illus. 46

Illus. 47

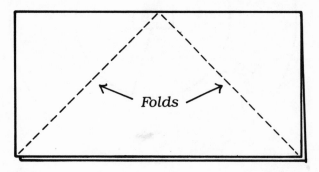

Folds

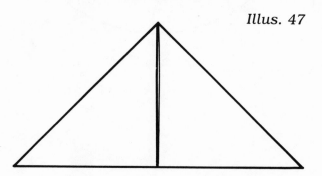

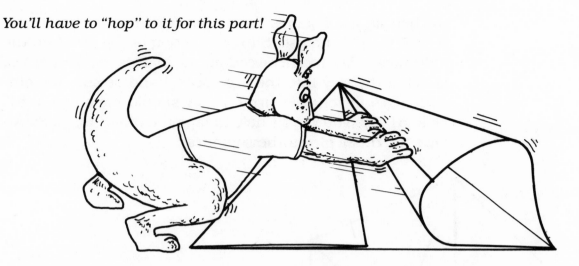

You'll have to "hop" to it for this part!

The next step is a little tricky. Look at Illus. 48. Lift the top layer at point A. This forms a triangular pocket. Make sure it opens all the way to point B. If it doesn't, stick your finger into the pocket and press up.

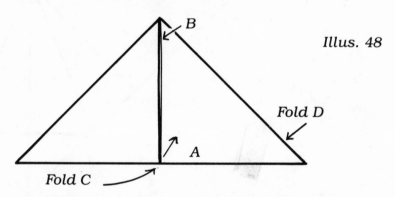

Illus. 48

When you open the pocket, push fold C into it as shown by the arrow. When fold C is directly above fold D, press it down and flatten out the pocket. With fold C tucked into the pocket, the fold should look like Illus. 49. Set this piece of paper aside and fold the other four pieces exactly the same way. Now the worst is over.

Illus. 49

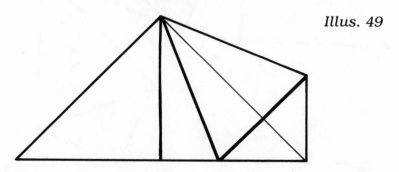

When all five squares have been folded, it is time to assemble your Pentadisc. Slip one section of the disc into the
little pocket of another section, as in Illus. 50. Push the
point all the way into the little pocket and be sure the outside edges fit together firmly. They should match Illus. 51.
Illus. 51 also shows you how to tape the pieces together. Attach the other pieces the same way.

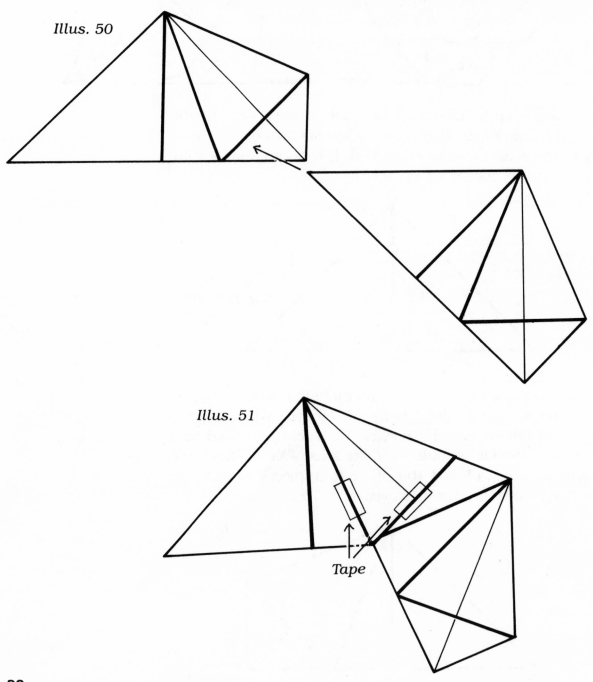

Illus. 50

Illus. 51

Tape

Make sure all the pointed ends are all the way at the end of the pocket in the other piece, and the outside edges of the point and the pocket are exactly together. Tape the pieces together as you work.

When you get ready to insert the final point, you will find it doesn't fit correctly, but don't worry—it's supposed to be that way. Push the final point into the last pocket—*all the way in*. When this happens, the outside edges of your Pentadisc will lift up. Press the final piece of tape firmly into place. Your Pentadisc is now high on the outside and low at the middle and looks like Illus. 52.

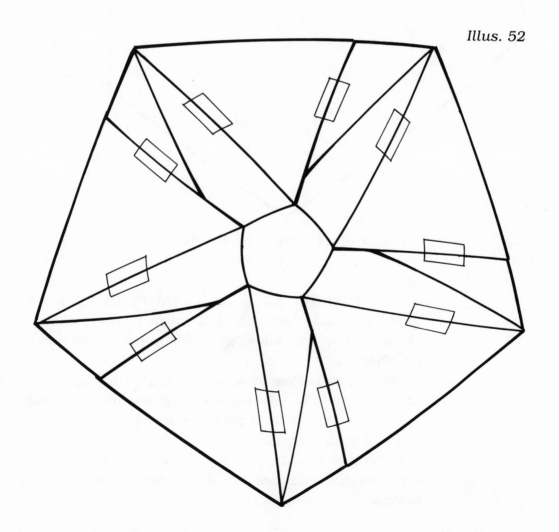

Illus. 52

Turn the disc over and tape down the five loose corners as shown in Illus. 53.

Illus. 53

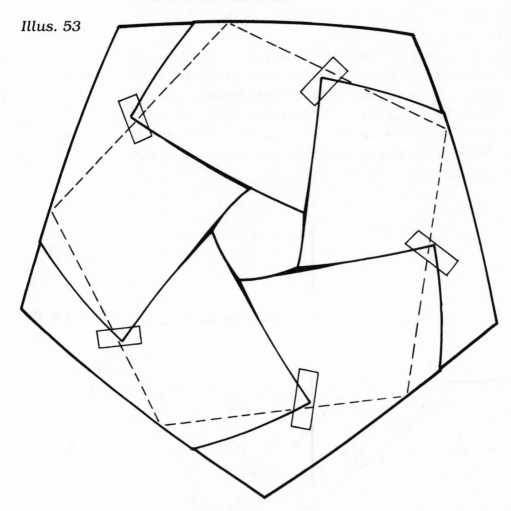

If you don't have tape handy for your disc and want to use glue, fine. It just takes a bit longer to wait for the glue to dry.

Now make the five folds shown by the dotted lines in Illus. 53. Fold them up and towards the middle. Crease them so that they stand straight up (or as close as you can get them).

Launch your Pentadisc with a fairly easy backhand snap of your wrist. It may not sail a great distance, but it will spin quite rapidly and maybe hover just a bit before coming in for an easy landing.

Experiment with different angles for the five points to see how the changes affect the way your disc sails and hovers.

After you have played with the Pentadisc you may want to make a smaller, indoor version. To make the smaller disc, use squares of paper which are only 5 inches on a side. The finished disc is small enough to safely launch in the house.

Octadisc

To make the Octadisc you need eight squares of notebook paper all the same size. Four-inch squares are good to start with.

Fold one paper square in half diagonally, along the dotted line in Illus. 54. Now fold along the dotted line in Illus. 55 so that the bottom point comes just to the top of the paper. Your paper should look like Illus. 56. Set this piece of paper aside and make the same folds in each of the other seven paper squares.

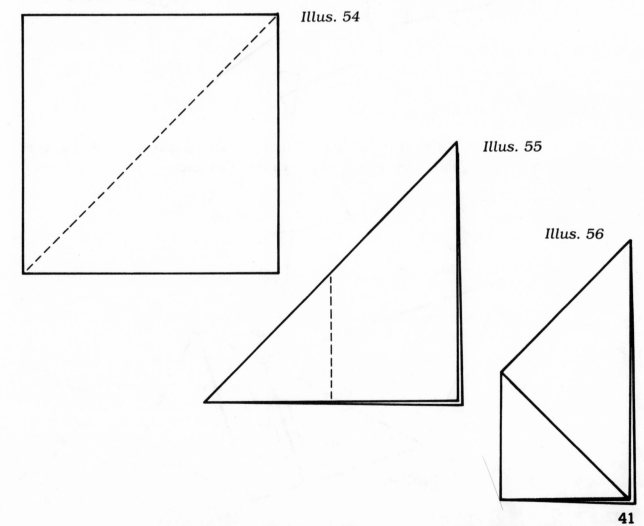

Illus. 54

Illus. 55

Illus. 56

Once all eight squares are folded, it is assembly time.

Look at Illus. 57. Slip the point of one folded piece into the triangular pocket (A) of another piece. Be sure to get the point all the way into the triangle.

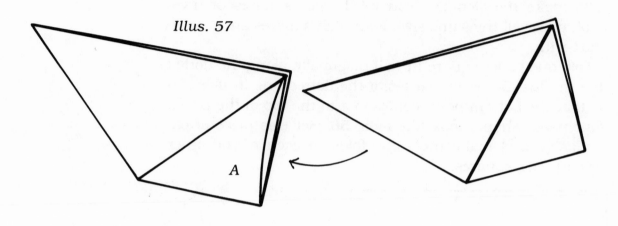

Illus. 57

Use a little strip of tape to hold the two pieces together. Illus. 58 shows where to put this tape.

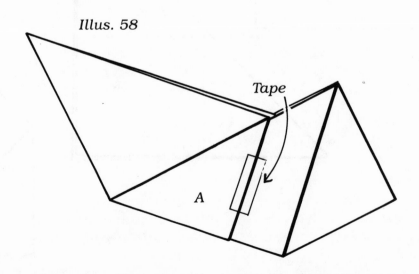

Illus. 58

Continue inserting the paper points and taping them into place. When you have everything taped together, your Octadisc looks like Illus. 59.

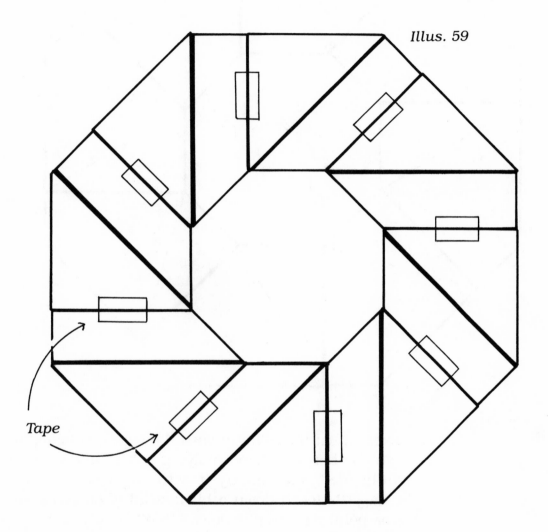

Illus. 59

Tape

Now turn your Octadisc over, so that it looks like Illus. 60. Make the folds shown by the eight dotted lines. Crease them well so that the flaps stand straight up; then turn the Octadisc back over so that the flaps are pointing down. Launch it with a quick backhanded flip and see what it does. This is one flying disc you can test indoors. It won't have a lot of distance but should give you some interesting flights.

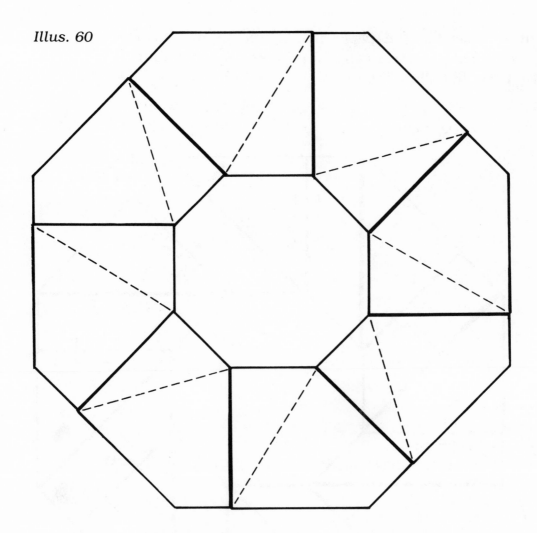

Illus. 60

Experiment by sailing it with the flaps on the top as well as on the bottom; then try flying it left-handed as well as right-handed. You can try it with larger squares, or with the flaps flattened down a bit instead of standing straight up or pointing straight down. Don't be afraid to try new things.

The Ring

Six paper plates can become a Ring with hardly any work.

Cut the central parts out of all six plates. Remember to be extremely careful not to poke yourself with the scissors. You're probably tired of hearing this, but it will really ruin your whole day if you stab through your finger as well as the plate.

Cut out the entire flat part of the paper plate (the darkened part in Illus. 61). Fit three of the paper plate rims inside one another. Use five or six strips of tape to hold them firmly together. Illus. 62 shows where to put the tape. The strip should be long enough to go all the way around the rings. Masking tape is really good but any tape will work.

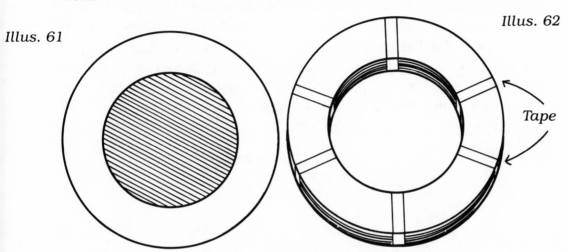

Illus. 61

Illus. 62

Tape

Now take just a minute and test-fly the half-ring. It won't do a bad job of flying.

Now stack the other three paper plates together just as you did before, and tape them in the same way.

Place the two rings together with the rims touching. Illus. 63 shows the Ring now. Use six strips of tape to fasten the two rings together tightly.

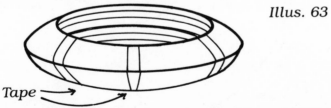

Illus. 63

Tape

Take the Ring outside and launch it with a backhand snap, just like the other flying discs. If there is a breeze blowing, toss the Ring with the wind. Most flying discs do not do their best when thrown against the wind.

You can also make an interesting Ring using only flat material. Cut four or five rings out of cereal boxes, and glue or tape them firmly together. This flat ring will sail much differently than the one made from paper plates. Try both Rings in various sizes.

The Saucer

This disc looks like a flying saucer from a science fiction movie. That's why it's called the Saucer.

Make the Saucer from either a paper plate or flat material such as the side of a cereal box. Don't use a plastic foam plate, because it won't work for this project.

Your first step is to draw circle A in Illus. 64. It should be 2 inches from the outer circle. On a paper plate, this is where the flat part meets the rim. If you are drawing your circles with a compass, set the pencil 2 inches from the outer edge of the plate. If you are using a round object to trace from, find one that's 4 inches shorter than the outer edge (since it has to come in 2 inches on either side).

Illus. 64

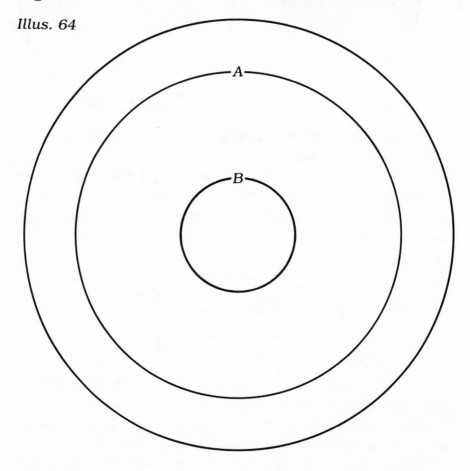

Now draw circle B about 1½ inches from the middle of the plate. The distance between circle A and circle B should be about 2 inches.

Now look at Illus. 65. Circle C is nearly halfway between circle A and B, so adjust your compass or round object to fit between A and B. But before you draw it, turn the paper plate over and draw it on the back.

Now comes the fun. When you make a deep crease in a piece of paper without cutting, you "score" it. Score the three circles on the sides on which you drew them. The best way to do this is with a dull table knife. Dull knives are just right for scoring.

Make sure you put a newspaper under the material when you score. This makes the scoring easier and also protects the top of the table or desk. If you don't use the newspaper or a piece of cardboard, you will make circles on the table top and that won't do anything but cause trouble.

Illus. 65

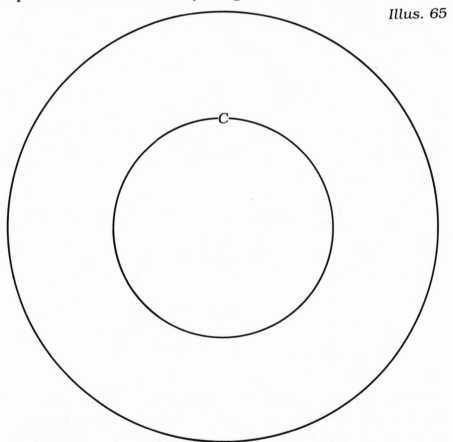

Hold the table knife down close to the tip of the blade and work slowly. Press straight down and move the knife point along the circle. If the point slips a bit, don't worry. Try to make perfect circles but don't get upset with little wobbles.

When you score the circles, cut out the section of material in Illus. 66. Cut both lines right to the middle of the plate with your scissors. Circle C is the dotted circle because it's on the other side of the plate.

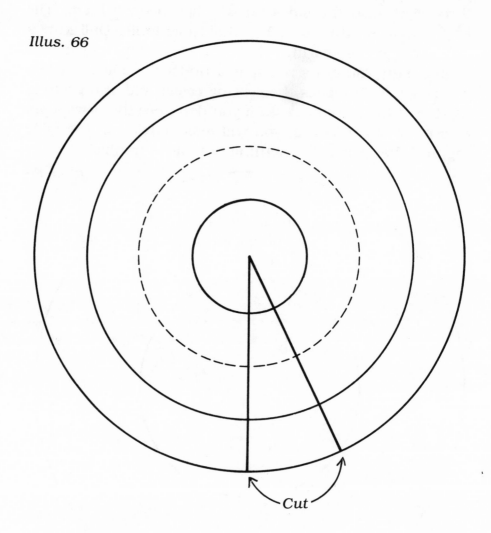

Illus. 66

Cut

Now you'll need about six hands and a lot of patience. Begin at the opening you just cut and start pushing down on circles A and B. Work just an inch at a time, and, as you're pushing down, push circle A towards circle B. This will make circle C rise between them.

As you work your way around the plate, circles A and B will bend down, circle C will lift up between them, and the middle part will also stand up just a bit.

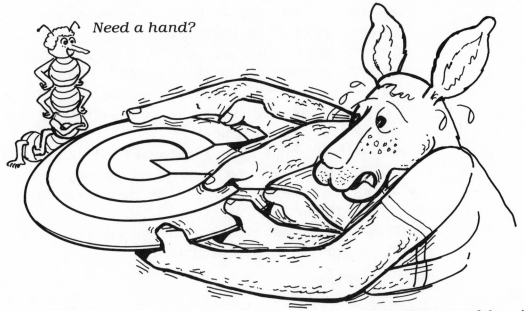

Need a hand?

I need about six of them!

When you have gone entirely around the circles, pull the edges together so that they overlap about half an inch or a little more. If a kink or fold develops in one of the circles, stop and press it into place. Staple the two sides together. (Two staples are a good idea. Illus. 67 shows where to put them.)

Illus. 67

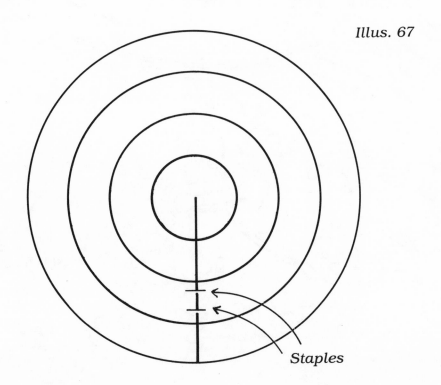

Staples

Tape or glue will also do the job, but you'll have to hold the Saucer together until the glue dries.

Turn the Saucer over and launch it with the bottom of the paper plate on top. It will turn over in flight.

A little weight may change your Saucer's flight. Slip a paper clip onto the rim; then slip on another one directly across from it. Test-fly it now.

Now, add two clips spaced between the first two so that you have a paper clip every quarter of the way around the Saucer's rim. This may improve your Saucer's flight. It may be a total disaster.

Try launching your Saucer a little faster than usual. This seems to improve its performance.

At least it flies!

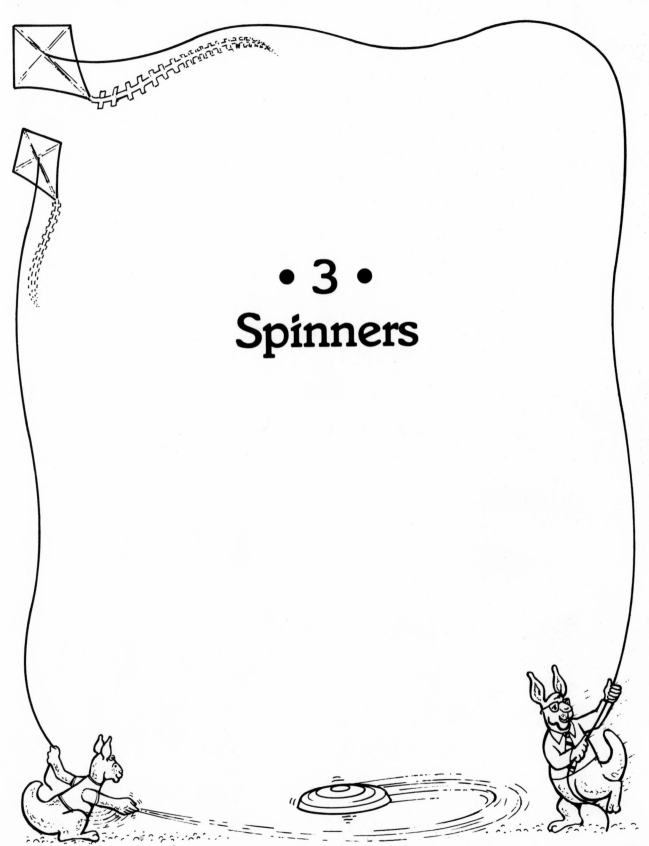

• 3 •
Spinners

Boomerang

Empty cereal boxes make great Boomerang material, and the best way to use one is to open it up flat. To do this, take your scissors and cut along the fold that has the double layer, so that this won't be part of your Boomerang. Open up the cereal box flat; then put it aside for just a minute.

Draw the design for your first Boomerang on a piece of notebook paper first, because it's easier to make changes on paper than on cardboard.

Boomerangs are coming back!

The basic Boomerang is shaped like Illus. 68. Illus. 69 shows an easy way to draw this shape.

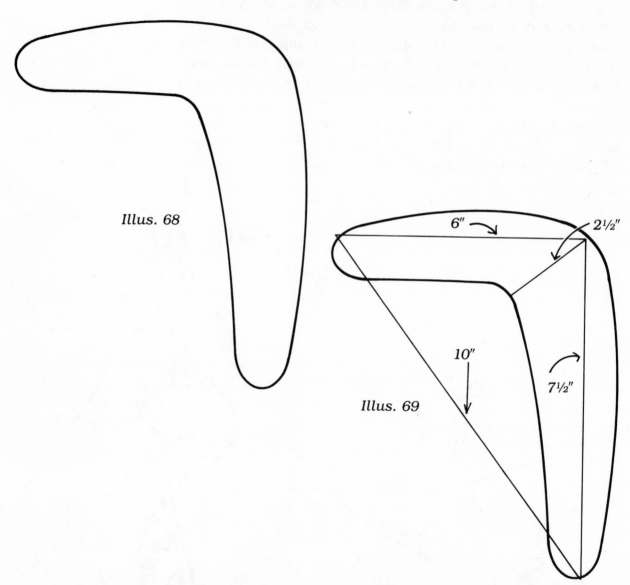

Illus. 68

Illus. 69

Lay out the triangle measurements in Illus. 69 on your paper. Do the 6-inch horizontal line first; then add the 8-inch vertical line. Connect these two lines with the diagonal line. It should be 10 inches, but it may be off a fraction of an inch; your Boomerang will still fly. Draw the 2¼-inch diagonal line so that it divides the angle you made right in the middle.

Sketch in the outline of the Boomerang around the lines you drew. It should match the shape in Illus. 69. Cut out the pattern so that you can trace it on the cardboard.

You'll need to make four copies of your Boomerang so that it will be strong enough to fly well. Draw your four shapes as you see them in Illus. 70. This way you'll fit all the layers onto one box. Don't worry if you are crossing over some folds because they won't be in the same place; so, when you glue your Boomerang together, it will be no problem.

Illus. 70

You deserve that for that joke!

Trace one copy of your Boomerang onto the cardboard and cut it out; then use it to trace the other three copies. It is lots easier to trace around the cardboard than it is around the paper.

Now glue the four layers together. Put a book or two on top of them while they dry. Once the glue is dry, your Boomerang is ready to sail.

You must go outside to fly your Boomerang. It will need plenty of room to get turned around and, even if you don't throw it very hard, it can easily go 100 feet or more, and can also sail as high as 50 feet. A lot of windows, vases, and lamps can get in its way, so test your Boomerang at a playground or in a park.

Illus. 71 shows how to hold the Boomerang correctly. Just pull your arm back and launch the Boomerang into the wind (if there is any). A combination side-arm and overarm throw seems to work best.

Throw your Boomerang high, because the higher it goes, the more likely it will reverse its direction and come back towards you.

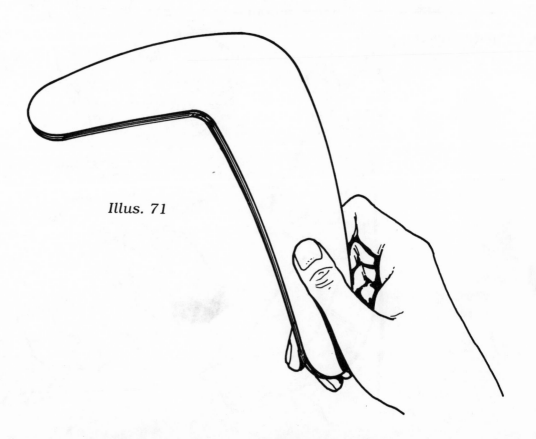

Illus. 71

Don't be discouraged if it does not come back the first time. Sometimes it takes a bit of practice to get just the right throw. Just remember to use a steep angle.

If your Boomerang gets caught in a tree or lands on a building, don't try to rescue it, because falling out of a tree or off the top of a house is no fun. The best thing to do when your Boomerang gets stuck is just to make another one with the pattern. With the pattern, it only takes a couple of minutes.

After you have flown your Boomerang a few times, try some different ideas. Try making one with arms of different lengths or one with one arm a lot wider than the other.

Some of your design changes may keep your Boomerangs from returning. When this happens, set up a box as a target and see if you can learn to hit it with your Boomerang. Don't worry if this wears the Boomerang out. You can always make a new one.

Flutter Fish

It takes about ten seconds to make a Flutter Fish. All you need is notebook paper and scissors.

Begin with a piece of paper about 8 inches long and 1 inch wide. Make the two cuts shown in Illus. 72.

Illus. 72

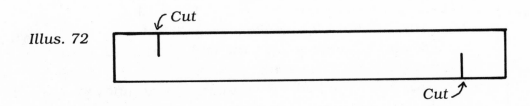

To assemble the Flutter Fish just pull one end over to the other end and interlock the two cuts. This is the figure in Illus. 73.

Illus. 73

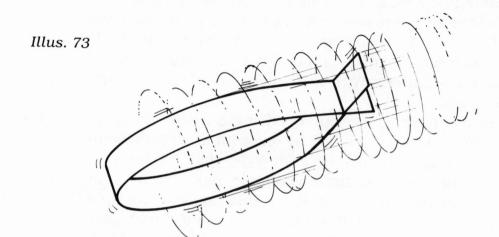

Illus. 74

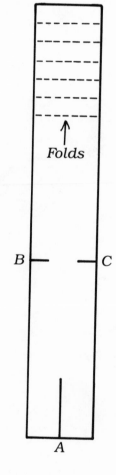

Hold the Flutter Fish up and let go. It will flutter to the ground twirling over and over. Little children love this, and if you have a cat, it will probably enjoy this flying toy no end.

Experiment with different-sized pieces of material until you discover the best Flutter Fish.

Chopper One

Begin with a piece of notebook paper 11 inches long and about 2 inches wide.

Look at Illus. 74. Make cut A about 1½ inches long. Move down 3 inches from the end of cut A and make cuts B and C, about ½ inch long each.

Now make the fold shown by the dotted lines in Illus. 74. Fold the end of the paper over about ½ inch; then fold it again and again. Each fold adds one layer of paper as you keep folding.

Illus. 75

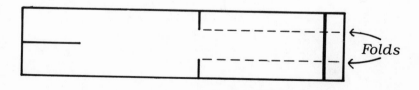

After your sixth fold your helicopter looks like Illus. 75. The dotted lines show your next two folds. Make these folds; then tuck one side under the other by slipping the right-hand side into the left-hand side. Separate the stack at the bottom from the top layer of paper on the left-hand side and slip the other side into that space. Your Chopper-to-be looks like Illus. 76.

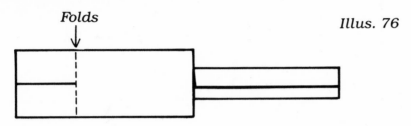

Folds

Illus. 76

To make the rotor blades, bend one blade forward on the dotted line shown in Illus. 76 and bend the other blade backwards. Make your rotors at about a 45° angle and you're ready to fly.

Toss your Chopper into the air. It should come to earth in a fast spin.

Experiment with the angle of the rotor blades. See if it will spin faster or slower as it falls.

Try making another helicopter which is either a bit narrower or a bit wider than the first one. Each change will make it fly just a little differently.

Wow! Just like on TV!

Chopper Two

Start with a piece of notebook paper 6 inches wide and 11 inches long. Fold it along the dotted lines in Illus. 77.

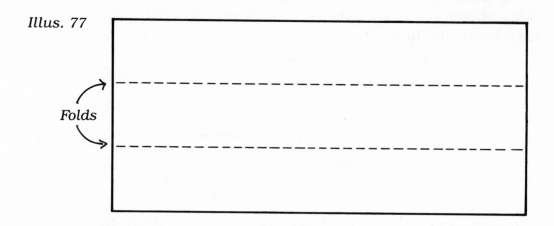

Illus. 77

Folds

Now make the three cuts in Illus. 78. Cut A is 1½ inches. Cuts B and C are each about ½ inch. Make them about 1 inch below the end of cut A.

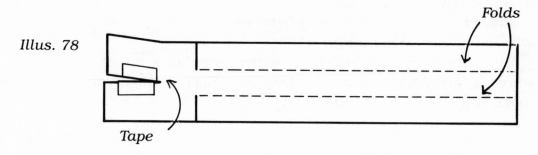

Folds

Illus. 78

Tape

Use two little pieces of transparent tape to keep the layers of paper from flapping when you fly your helicopter. Illus. 78 shows where to put them. Fold the tape around the cut edges to hold all three layers of paper together.

Illus. 78 also shows two dotted lines. Make the two folds along these lines so that they match Illus. 79.

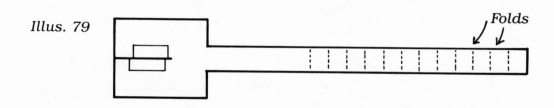

Illus. 79

Folds

Illus. 79 shows the next folds. Keep on folding the paper over onto itself until you only have 2 inches left to fold. You can see this in Illus. 80. Use a strip of tape to hold this roll of material in place.

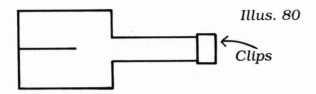

Illus. 80

Clips

Bend the two rotor arms just as you did for Chopper One so that one points forward and the other points backwards.

Test Chopper Two outside by tossing it as high as you can. If it does not fall fast enough to create a good spin, you can add a paper clip or two just above the thick roll of material at the bottom.

Chopper Three

To begin Chopper Three you need a piece of material from a cereal box. If you have some left over from your Boomerang, use that. Cut a piece 2 inches by 9 inches.

Now, make the cuts shown in Illus. 81. Cut A is about 2 inches long and cuts B and C are about ⅝ inch deep each.

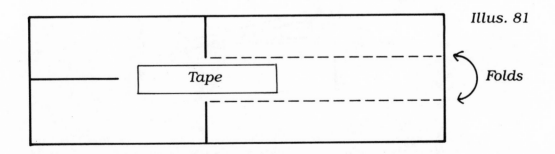

Illus. 81

Tape

Folds

Note the tape in Illus. 81. This is to make Chopper Three strong enough to fly outdoors. Tape both sides of the material. Masking tape is great but transparent tape is fine as well. Several layers certainly won't hurt.

After putting the tape in place make the folds along the dotted lines in Illus. 81. Fold one side forward and the other back to give it the proper balance. Wrap two strips of tape around the folded cardboard to hold it in place. Illus. 82 shows where to put it.

Illus. 82

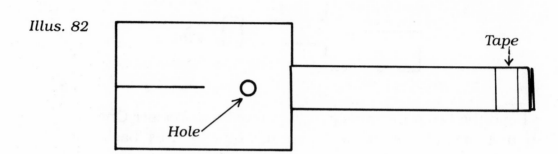

Next, make the hole shown in Illus. 82. A paper punch can do it well. Otherwise, poke the hole with the point of a pair of scissors, without poking your hand or finger, or the table top.

Bend the rotor blades so that one extends forward and the other back.

Cut one side of a rubber band so that you have a long single strand of rubber. Staple one end to one rotor arm as in Illus. 83.

Illus. 83

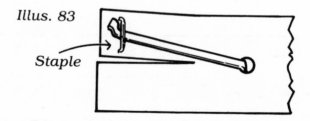

Run the other end through the hole and staple it to the second rotor blade. The rubber band should pull the rotor arms down at about a 45° angle. If the rubber band is too short it will pull the blades too far down, and if the band is too long it won't pull the rotors into place, and you know what that means: improper spin.

Bend a paper clip so that it looks like Illus. 84.

Illus. 84

Slip one end under the tape at the nose. Wrap another strip of tape around the base of the clip so that it won't fall out while in flight. It should look like Illus. 85.

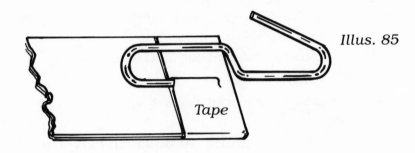

Illus. 85

Tape

Now you have to make a launcher. Fold a sheet of notebook paper in half the long way; then begin rolling it tightly from one end until you form a roll of paper about 4½ inches long.

Double this roll in the middle and slip a rubber band into the bend. Then wrap a strip of tape around the two ends to hold things together. The launcher looks like Illus. 86.

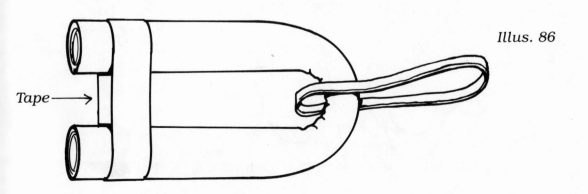

Illus. 86

Tape ——→

Take Chopper Three outside. Hold the launcher in one hand. Hook the loose end of the paper clip into the rubber band. Grasp the helicopter between your thumb and index finger by taking hold of the rotor blades. When you do this, it stretches the rubber band stapled to the rotor blades.

Hold the helicopter firmly and pull the launcher forward (away from you). When the launcher's rubber band is stretched about 8 inches, let go of the Chopper. It will snap into the air.

At the top of its flight, the rubber band will pull the rotor blades into position and your helicopter will spin to the ground.

Experiment until you find just how far to stretch the launcher's rubber band. If the rubber band breaks, just replace it. If the Chopper tears, either tape it together or make a new one.

Hang on to your launcher. You'll need it for some other flying toys.

Whirly Cone

It takes about a minute to build this great outdoor toy.

It's fun to fly, but ___ eat!

Roll a sheet of notebook or typing paper into a cone as shown in Illus. 87. Tightly close the small end of the cone, and hold it in shape with a short piece of transparent tape.

Use your scissors to cut down about 2 inches every ½ inch or so around the rim of the cone. These cuts are shown in Illus. 87.

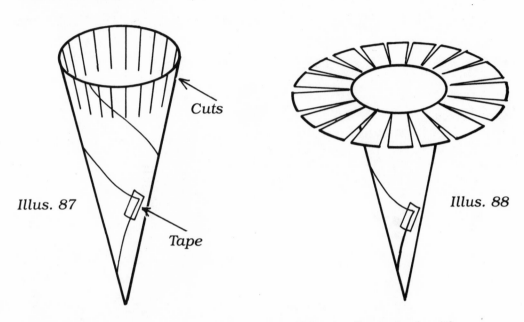

Cuts

Illus. 87

Tape

Illus. 88

Bend down the cuts so that your Whirly Cone looks like Illus. 88.

Drop a small rock into the end of the cone for weight. Throw the Whirly Cone as high as you can into the air. It will come spinning down to the ground.

Experiment with the folds. Try bending part of them straight down to see how this changes the spins; then try bending these tips up.

Only he'd try to eat it!

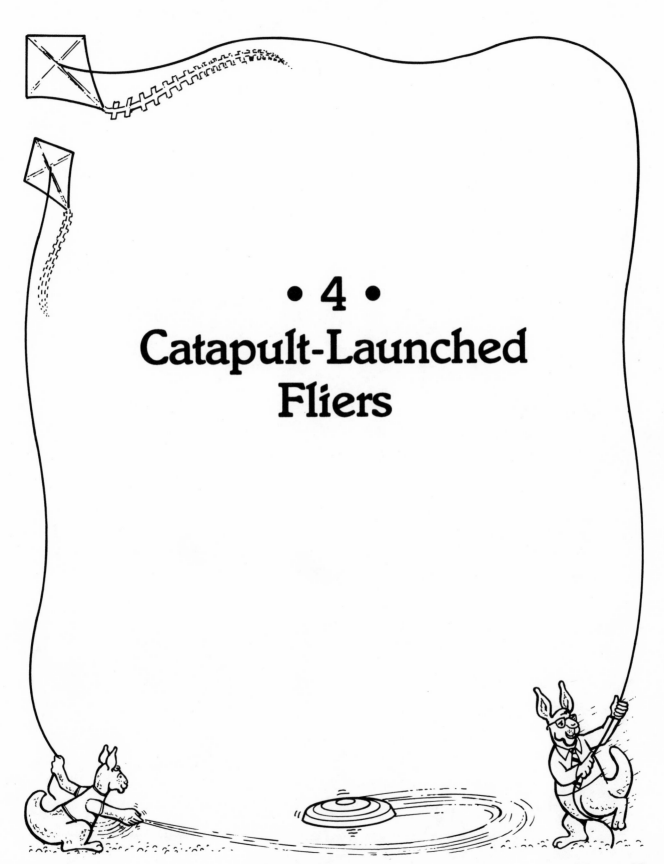

• 4 •
Catapult-Launched
Fliers

A catapult fires missiles into the air. In olden days catapults hurled rocks at castle walls and everyone involved was likely to get hurt. Your catapults won't hurt anyone, but you should have a lot of fun with them.

The catapult you'll be using for some of these projects is the same one you used for Chopper Three.

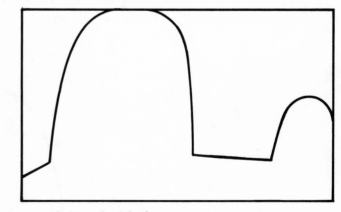

Good thing I didn't

throw it away!

Dizzy

A 4 × 6-inch file card is ideal for Dizzy. Fold the card in half the long way as in Illus. 89.

Draw an outline for Dizzy as shown in Illus. 90. Try to match it as closely as possible. Don't worry if it's a little off.

Illus. 89

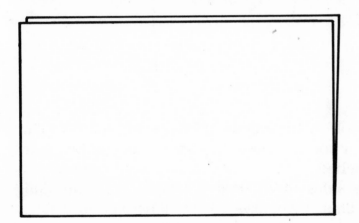

Illus. 90

Cut Dizzy out of the file card, but be careful to hold the two sides of the card together firmly. If one side slips, Dizzy will come out with wings of different shapes and we don't want that.

Now slip a paper-clip launching hook between the layers at the plane's nose. Tape it firmly into place with several layers of tape as shown in Illus. 91. Masking tape works really well but any tape will do the job.

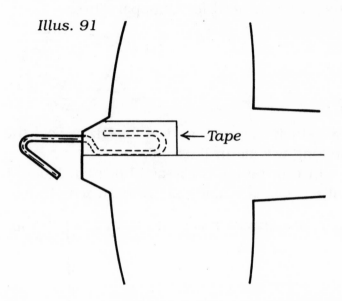

Illus. 91

Bend the hook in front down a bit, as in Illus. 91. This makes it easier for the hook to slip off the rubber band when it's launched.

Tape Dizzy's sides together at the nose, tail, and along the fuselage. Illus. 92 shows where. (Fuselage is a fancy word for the body of the airplane.) After taping the fuselage, fold down the wings and tail section so that they stick straight out.

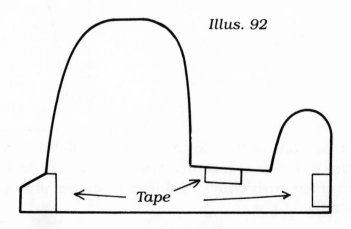

Illus. 92

Fold the tips of Dizzy's wings up along the dotted lines in Illus. 93. These are vertical stabilizers, since they're vertical and they keep the plane stable.

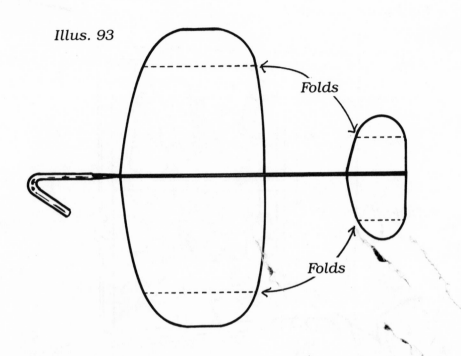

Illus. 93

Folds

Folds

Do the same for the tail section. The dotted lines show where to make the folds. The tail is a horizontal stabilizer, except for the folded ends, which are vertical stabilizers, obviously.

Now slip the hook over the rubber band on the launcher. Pull back a bit and let Dizzy sail into the air. Don't pull back too far the first time or two. Take it easy until you see how Dizzy performs.

When a paper airplane stalls, the solution is usually quite simple—slip a paper clip onto the nose and launch it again.

Try and keep in mind that all catapult-launched airplanes should be flown outside. Some of them really take off and go, and there is just not room for them inside a house or apartment. When you're outside, watch out for trees and buildings. If a tree gobbles up your flying toy or the top of a building becomes a landing field, don't try a rescue. Just leave it until the wind blows it down, or, better yet, make a new model.

Never launch one of these flying toys towards anyone. They fly very fast when they leave the launcher, and the launching hook is not something anyone wants to have hit him in the face. Keep these things in mind and everyone will have fun.

OOOPS!!

After you have flown Dizzy successfully, you may want to come up with other kinds of airplanes—ones with big wings, small wings or whatever you can imagine!

High Flier

To build your High Flier you need a sheet of notebook paper and two 4 × 6-inch file cards, or any stiff material. It needs to be fairly light as well as stiff, which is why file cards work so well.

Roll the paper into a hollow tube 11 inches long and about ½ inch across. Tape it where shown in Illus. 94 to keep it from unrolling.

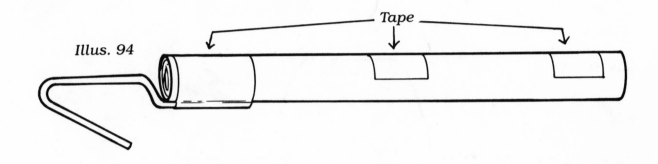

Illus. 94   Tape

Put one end of the launching hook at one end of the tube, and then wrap several layers of tape around the hook to hold it in place. This is now the nose of your High Flier.

Fold one of the 4 × 6 cards in half; then draw half a wing. It should look like Illus. 95. Make sure you hold the two sides of the card firmly together when you cut out the wing.

Illus. 95

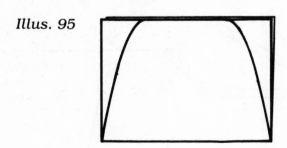

Tape the wing onto the fuselage so that the front is about 1½ inches from the tip of the nose. Illus. 96 shows where.

Turn High Flier over and run a strip of tape along each side of the fuselage. Transparent tape is best because it is so light.

To get the tape into the space between the wing and the fuslage, fold it double with the sticky side out; then press the fold as far as you can into this space. Illus. 97 shows where to put these strips.

Illus. 96

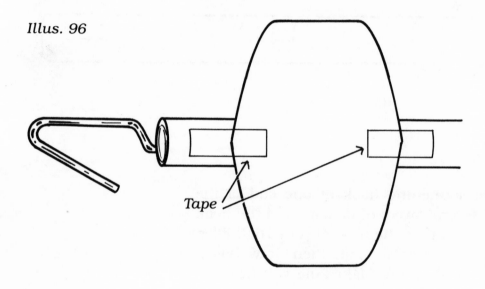

Tape

Illus. 97

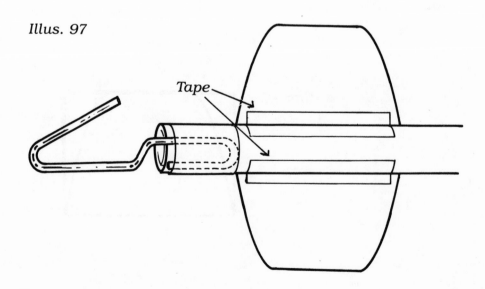

Tape

Now fold the other file card in half. Draw the tail section ("the horizontal stabilizer," if you want to sound like a pilot) as shown in Illus. 98. The two little tabs at the front and back will make it easier to tape the stabilizer onto the fuselage.

Mount the horizontal stabilizer so that the rear tab meets the end of the fuselage, as shown in Illus. 99. Wrap a strip of tape around both tabs. This will hold the horizontal stabilizer in place during even the roughest flights or hardest landings.

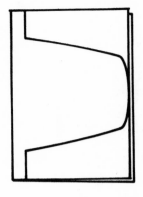

Illus. 98

Illus. 99

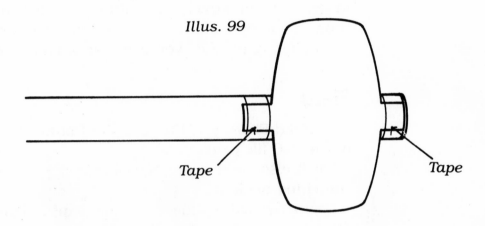

Tape

Tape

Fold up the tips of the wing and horizontal stabilizer along the dotted lines in Illus. 100. When this is done, your High Flier is ready for its first test flight.

Illus. 100

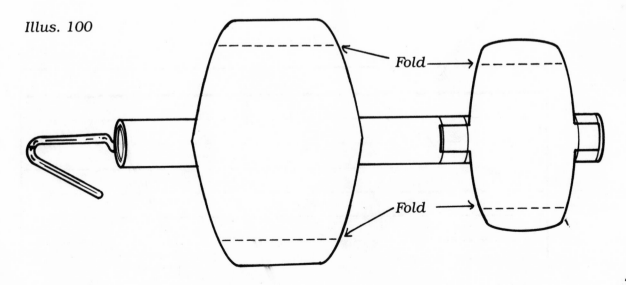

Fold

Fold

Fold

Slip the launching hook over the rubber band on the catapult launcher and pull back. Don't try for great distance on the first flight. Just give the rubber band a little pull and see how your High Flier performs.

If you have any problems with the launching hook getting tangled with the rubber band, try bending the hook out a little bit or holding the launcher differently. Be sure the rubber band is right at the end and well away from your fingers. If your High Flier stalls in flight, just add a paper clip or two to the nose.

High Flier will sail for quite a distance, but if it happens to get into the street, wait until it is safe to rescue it. If your rescue operation is too late and you have a flattened High Flier, remember, you can just build a new one.

Flaps

To build Flaps, you'll need a sheet of notebook paper and two 4 × 6 file cards.

You'll also need some tape and a paper clip to make a launching hook.

Begin by folding the notebook paper along the dotted line you see in Illus. 101. Fold over the paper's edge ½ inch; then fold it over again. Fold over the whole paper. Fasten the loose edge with three little strips of tape so that it won't unfold.

Illus. 101

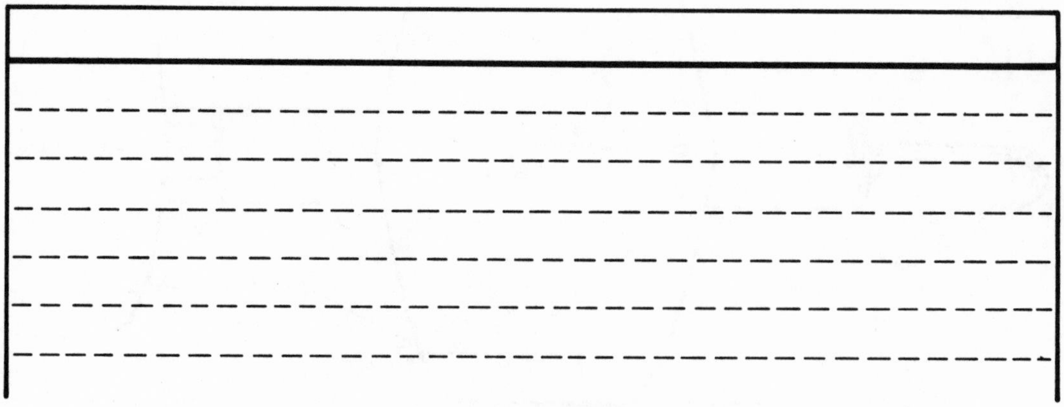

Wrap several layers of tape around the nose. Slip one end of the launching hook under the tape layers; then wrap several more layers of tape around the hook to hold it in place. Illus. 102 shows how Flaps should look at this point. Twist the launching hook's free end half a turn so that it hangs down below the flat part of the fuselage.

Illus. 102

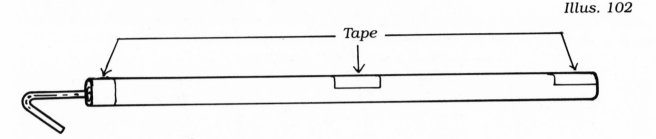

Tape

Now fold both file cards double. Draw the wing outline exactly like the one in Illus. 103. Cut the wing out and tape it onto the fuselage. Put the front edge of the wing (pilots call this the leading edge) about 1¼ inches from the tip of the nose.

Use two strips of tape to fasten the wing to the fuselage; then turn Flaps over and use two strips of tape on the underside of the wing.

Draw the tail piece on the other folded file card to match Illus. 104. Cut it out and tape it onto the fuselage so that the rear tab of material is even with the rear of the fuselage. Wrap a strip of tape around both the front and rear tabs.

Illus. 103   *Illus. 104*

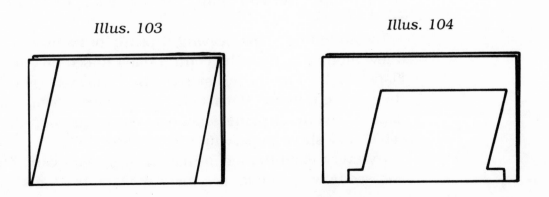

Flaps should now look like Illus. 105. Fold up the wings and stabilizers at the dotted lines. Crease them so that they stand straight up and act as vertical stabilizers.

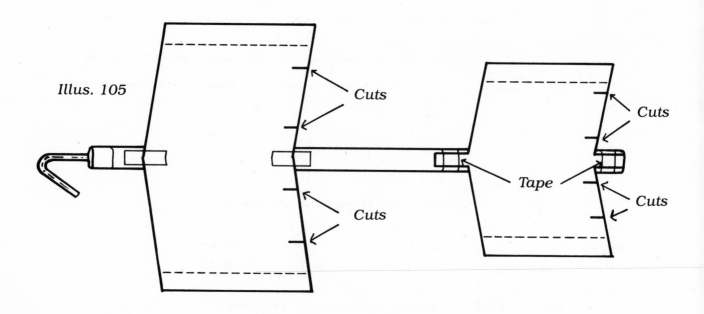

Illus. 105

In Illus. 105, you also see eight cuts in the rear edges of the wing and tail piece. (Pilots call these rear edges "trailing edges.") Make all eight cuts about ⅜ inch long. Bend up the material between each pair of cuts. These are now control flaps. You can adjust them to change the way your airplane flies.

Try launching Flaps, leaving it plenty of room to fly. After a few flights, change the control flaps to see how it affects Flaps's flight. Put the left side up, and the right side down; then switch them. With both wing flaps down and tail flaps up, your airplane should make a big loop. If Flaps stalls, just slip a paper clip over its nose.

Try every combination of flap settings you can think of and see how each changes the way Flaps performs.

Sky Looper

A cereal box becomes a Sky Looper with just a bit of fold-ing and a few cuts.

Save up those cereal boxes!

Cut out a side from the box to get started. Draw a line right down the middle of the material as shown in Illus. 106. Now you need to score that line so that you can fold it without getting a bunch of little wrinkles. (If you forget how to score a piece of cardboard, check back on page 47.)

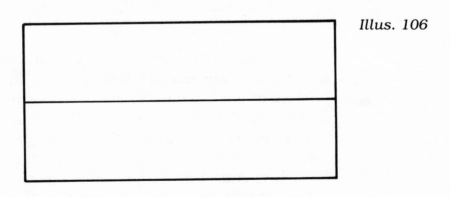

Illus. 106

Fold the cardboard along the scored line, and draw the outline you see in Illus. 107. Use the measurements in Illus. 107 to guide you when you draw this outline. If it's a little different don't worry about it, but try to come pretty close.

Illus. 107

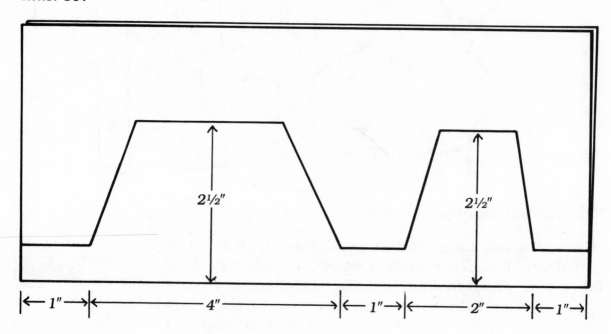

Be very careful when you cut out your Sky Looper because you are cutting through two thicknesses of cardboard at once. If your scissors are not up to the task, then just unfold the cardboard and cut out just the side you drew. Refold the cardboard and trace around the side you cut out. This gives you a pattern for the second side.

When your Sky Looper is cut out, slip the launching hook inside the nose between the two layers of material. Tape it firmly into place; then fold the airplane along its central fold and tape it as shown in Illus. 108. Be sure to wrap the tape all the way around the fuselage a time or two.

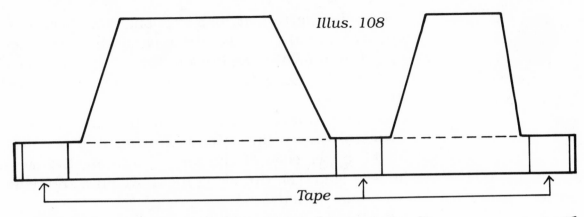

Illus. 108

Tape

Illus. 109

The dotted lines in Illus. 108 show where to bend the wing and horizontal stabilizer down. Bend them only about ⅔ of the way down. Illus. 109 shows how the wings and stabilizer should look head-on. This gives the plane "dihedral," which is pilot talk for the angle of the wing.

Before you make your first launch, slip two or three paper clips onto the airplane's nose. Don't worry if they extend lower than the bottom of the fuselage. You may put as many as five or six clips onto the nose because the cardboard is very heavy in relation to the wing area and Sky Looper is likely to stall without lots of nose weight.

It doesn't look like a cereal box!

Streak

It only takes a few minutes to turn a 4 × 6 card into Streak. In addition to the file card you will need a ruler, a rubber band, a large cereal box, and the tape, the paper clips, and the scissors.

Fold the file card in half the long way. This is a quick way to locate the middle of the card. Measure ½ inch out each way from the middle and mark the points as shown in Illus. 110. Use these points to draw the two dotted lines in Illus. 110.

Locate two points that are 2 inches along either side of the card. Draw a line from each point to the central point at the upper edge of the card. These are the two dotted lines in Illus. 111. Cut along these two lines and remove the dark areas in Illus. 111.

Fold the material along its central crease already in place; then fold the material down on the two lines you first drew.

Illus. 110

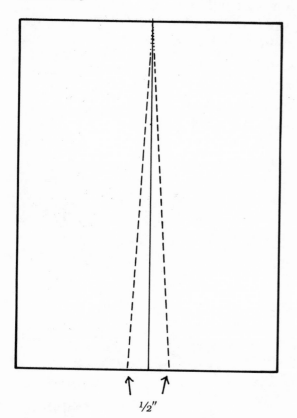

½"

Illus. 111

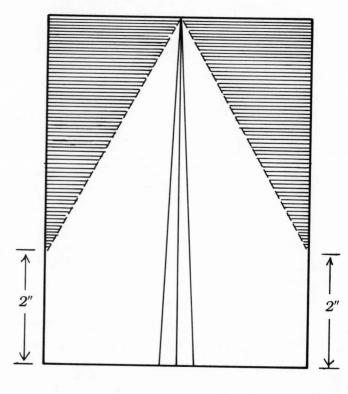

2"

2"

After folding Streak's wings down into place, fold up on the dotted lines in Illus. 112. These folds are about ¼ inch from the edge of the material.

Bend a paper clip into the launching hook in Illus. 113. This launching hook is a little different from the ones you made for the other planes.

Poke a hole through the central fold with the hook 1 inch back from Streak's nose point. This leaves most of the paper clip in the central fold with only the launching hook sticking through the material. Be sure the hook points towards Streak's tail. Tape the launching hook firmly in place along the inside of the central fold.

Illus. 112

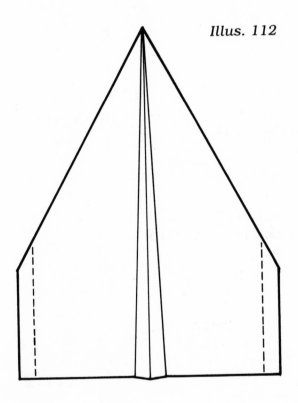

Illus. 113

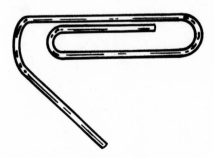

Use a short piece of tape to hold Streak's tail section together firmly. Use another strip of tape along the craft's top above the launching hook to make sure the central fold stays folded. Illus. 114 shows where to put the tape.

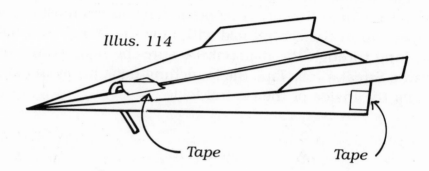

Illus. 114

Tape

Tape

Slip two or three paper clips onto Streak's nose and hand-launch the aircraft. Once you have the proper of number of clips in place, Streak should sail in an even glide path.

Now cut a rubber band so that you have a single strand of rubber. Wrap a strip of tape around each end of the rubber band several times, but leave a tail of tape about 2 inches long. It should look like Illus. 115.

Illus. 115

Now tape both ends of the rubber band to a large cereal box, as in Illus. 116. Be sure the tape is stuck firmly to the sides of the box. Add a little more tape to each side to make sure it stays down.

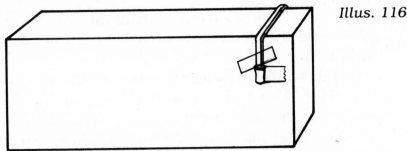

To launch Streak, slip the launching hook into the rubber band. Pull Streak back by grasping its tail firmly. Be sure to pull the airplane back along the side of the cereal-box launching pad. Aim the side of the box upwards at a little angle and let go of Streak's tail.

Streak should take off like a shot and sail 20 or 30 feet without any effort. This is why Streak is best launched outside. If it catches just the right breeze, Streak will surprise you with the length and speed of its flights.

Experiment with the best launch angle and with how far to pull back on the rubber band. Try different-size Streaks. Whatever you experiment with should make a fantastic flier.

R. S. C. Ninja

R. S. C. is an engineering student, and when he's not in class or studying, he's making paper airplanes. He built the Ninja especially for this book.

Begin with a sheet of notebook or typing paper. Fold up the bottom edge about 2 inches so that your paper looks like Illus. 117.

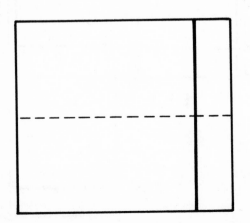

Illus. 117

Now make the middle fold along the dotted line in Illus. 117. Leave the Ninja folded that way so that it looks like Illus. 118.

Fold down the side nearer to you along the dotted line in Illus. 118. Then turn the airplane over and fold the other side down the same way.

Unfold these folds so that your Ninja looks like Illus. 119. The middle fold forms a little mountain in the middle of the paper. Fold over both top corners along the dotted lines in Illus. 119. Make sure that the folds go to the edges of the paper beside the middle fold but not to the middle fold. Your R. S. C. Ninja is now shown in Illus. 120. The dotted lines indicate your next folds. Once again, fold the edges of the paper to the fold lines beside the middle fold, not to the middle fold itself.

Illus. 118

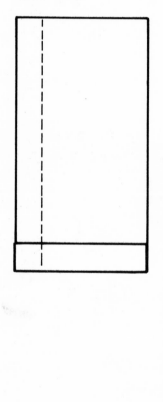

Illus. 119

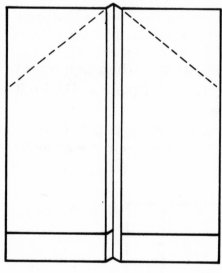

Illus. 120

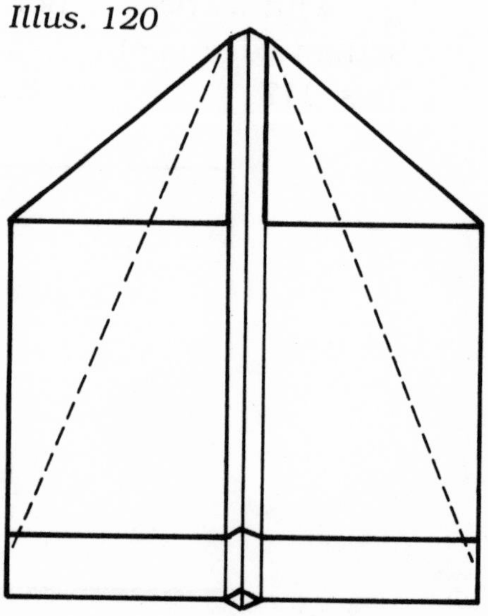

Turn your airplane over. It should look like Illus. 121. The middle fold is now a little valley in the middle of the paper. Fold both sides along the dotted lines in Illus. 121; then press several layers of tape onto the tail area. Tape both the bottom and the top of the airplane.

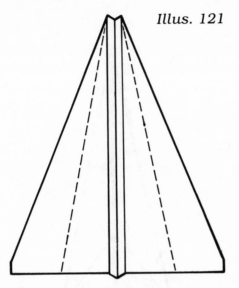

Illus. 121

Slip a rubber band onto a paper clip, but don't bend the clip! The band and clip should look like Illus. 122.

Slip the paper clip over the taped tail section of your airplane. Make sure the clip is in the valley of the middle fold. The rubber band should be at the front of the clip so that it points towards the airplane's nose, as seen in Illus. 123.

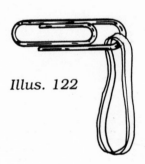

Illus. 122

This is a good time to slip two paper clips over the front of the folded wings. Illus. 123 shows where.

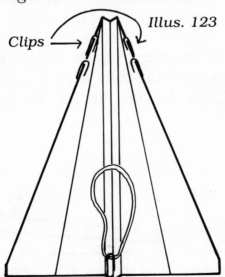

Clips ⟶

Illus. 123

Turn the airplane over and fasten the wings together with tape. Place the tape as you see in Illus. 124. Make sure the wings are not pulled together too tightly. Leave about ⅛ inch of space between the wings.

Illus. 124

It is now launch time. First, launch your R. S. C. Ninja by hand. If it does not glide pretty evenly, experiment with the nose paper clips until it glides in an even path. It may not fly far, but the important thing is that it does not stall or hesitate in flight.

Now you need the ruler. Slip the loose end of the rubber band over the end of the ruler as seen in Illus. 125. Make certain the edge of the ruler fits into the airplane's central fold.

Pull here

Illus. 125

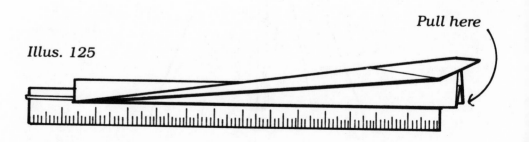

Grasp the tail section firmly between your thumb and index finger and pull back. Hold the ruler steady with your other hand. Keep the airplane's middle fold firmly along the ruler's edge.

Let go of the tail and watch your R. S. C. Ninja fly off its launching catapult. It should really get out and go!

Practise launching the airplane so that you always hold its central fold right along the ruler's edge. Pull back a bit more on the rubber band until you find just the right amount of pull needed to give your airplane its best flight.

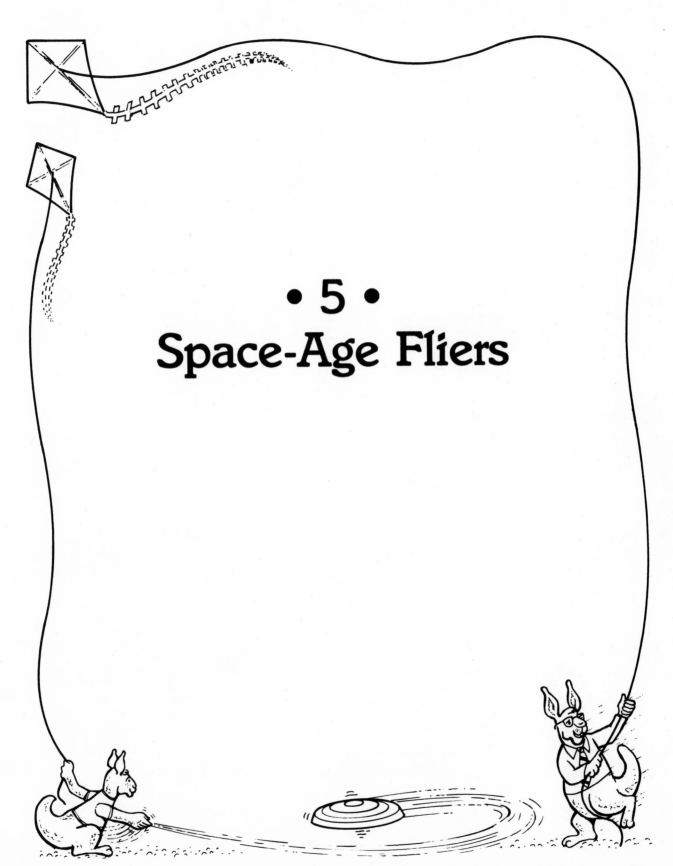

• 5 •
Space-Age Fliers

The flying paper toys in this chapter are right out of the space age in design. They all glide differently since all have different designs.

Lunar Explorer

Cut a sheet of notebook or typing paper in half so that you have a piece of material which is about $5\frac{1}{2} \times 8\frac{1}{2}$ inches. Turn it so that the long side is in front of you as you see in Illus. 126. Fold the paper in half to make a fold down the middle; then unfold the paper so that it lies flat.

Illus. 126

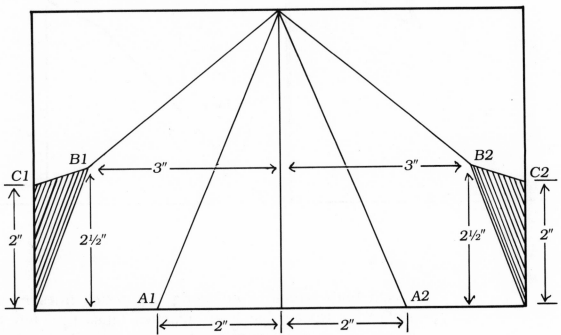

Now to do some measuring and drawing.

Measure 2 inches on either side of the middle fold and make dots to locate point A1 and point A2; then draw the lines from these points to the nose point of Lunar Explorer.

Now measure from the middle 3 inches out and $2\frac{1}{2}$ inches up from the tail on each side. This is where point B1 and point B2 are located. Draw the two lines from these points to the nose point of the craft.

Next, measure up from the tail along the outside edges exactly 2 inches, and mark point C1 and point C2 on either side of Lunar Explorer. Connect B1 to C1 and B2 to C2 on both wings; then draw lines from points B down to the corners.

In Illus. 126 the area between these lines is blacked out because these sections of material are going to be cut out.

Fold the airplane along its central fold so that it looks like Illus. 127. Fold down the wings along the dotted lines for both sides of Lunar Explorer. After these folds it looks like Illus. 128.

Illus. 127

Illus. 128

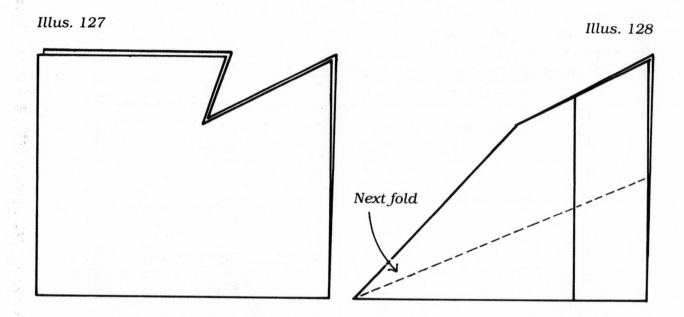

Next fold

Fold both wings down along the dotted lines in Illus. 128. Your Space Age Flier matches Illus. 129. Lift both wings up into position so that they extend straight out from the fuselage.

Illus. 129

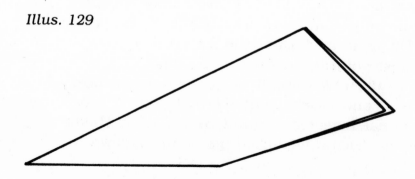

Slip two paper clips onto the fuselage. Illus. 130 shows where. These will give Lunar Explorer the proper trim, and also hold it together in flight.

Illus. 130

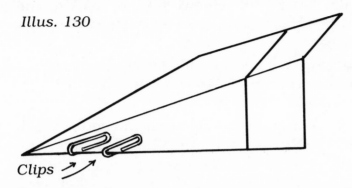

Clips

Launch this aircraft with a quick overhand snap of your wrist. If it is trimmed correctly, it will glide in a long, even path.

These projects really are "far out"!

Alien Interceptor

You need a full sheet of typing or notebook paper to build this project. You also need a ruler, a pair of scissors, some transparent tape, and a pencil.

Fold the paper in the middle the long way, so that you have a central line from which to measure. Once this fold is made, unfold the paper so that it lies flat.

Measure 2½ inches to the right of the fold along the bottom of the paper. Mark that location point A1. You can see this in Illus. 131. Now locate point A2, which is 2½ inches to the left. Draw lines connecting points A to the middle point at the other end of the paper. That is the Alien Interceptor nose.

Measure up 4 inches along side of the paper, and mark these points B1 and B2. Connect these points with the aircraft's nose as in Illus. 131.

Next, measure up 8 inches from the bottom of the paper along either side. Mark these locations points C1 and C2, and join them with the nose point.

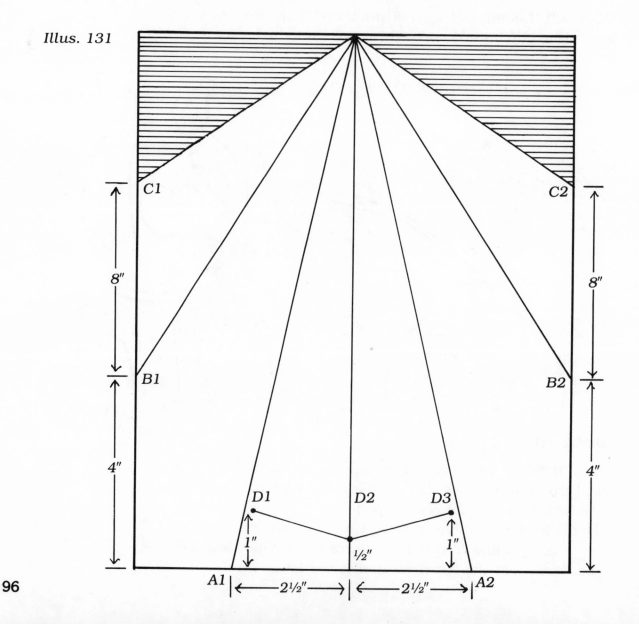

Illus. 131

Now, measure up from the tail ½ inch along the fold; then measure up from the tail 1 inch along the lines drawn from points A1 and A2. Connect these points and label them D1, D2 and D3, as in Illus. 131.

You are now ready to cut and fold Alien Interceptor.

Cut out the darkened areas in Illus. 131. Just cut from C1 and C2 to the top of the fold. Turn the paper over and fold along lines B1 and B2 towards the middle. Illus. 132 shows these folds. Note that the edge of the paper does not quite reach the middle.

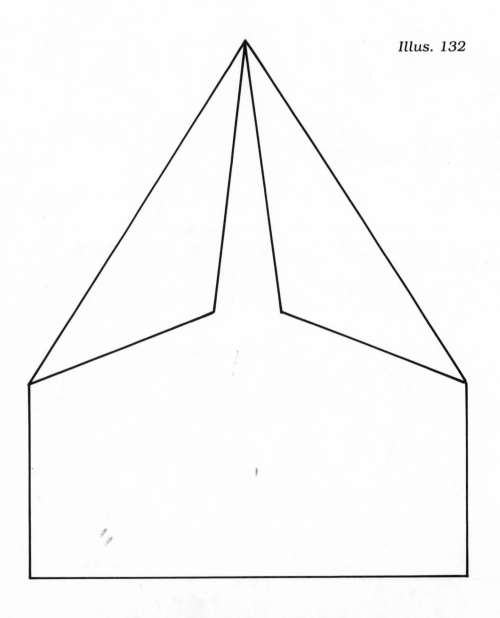

Illus. 132

Fold the paper up along the central fold so that it looks like Illus. 133. You also see where to make a cut. This is the line that connects D1, D2 and D3. Cut along this line, but be careful because you are cutting through two thicknesses of paper.

Illus. 133

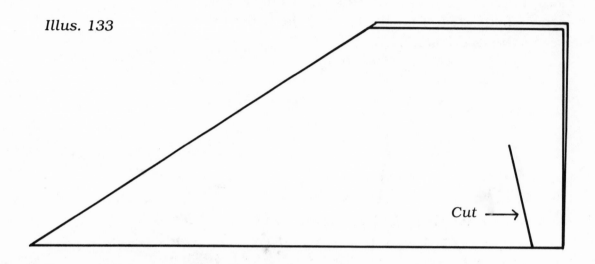

Cut ⟶

Hold the tail section at the arrow in Illus. 133. Push this cut area upwards until it folds itself inside out and looks like Illus. 134.

Illus. 134

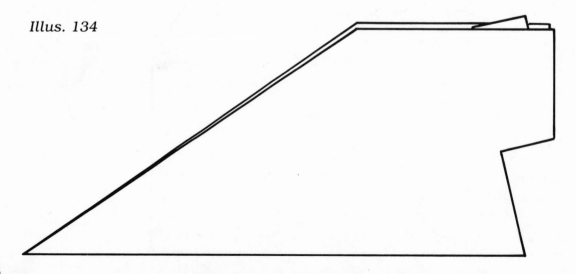

Now fold both wings down along lines A1 and A2 so that your aircraft matches Illus. 135.

Illus. 135

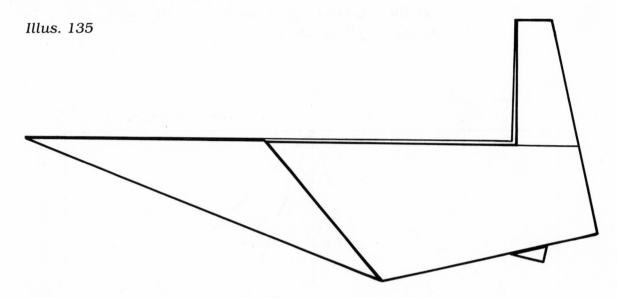

Pull the wings up so that they extend straight out from the fuselage; then lift them another ¼ inch. Use a short strip of transparent tape to hold the wings in this position. Illus. 136 shows where to put it.

Illus. 136

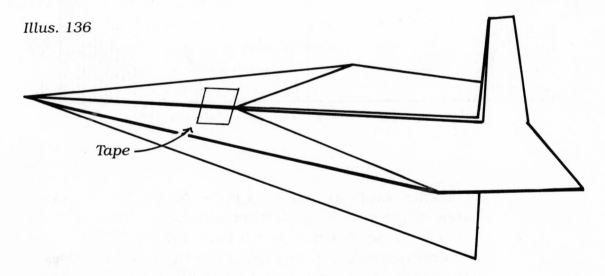

Tape

Slip two or three paper clips onto your Alien Interceptor's nose and give it a test launch.

When trimming with paper clips, it sometimes helps to move one of the clips backwards or forward until you get the perfect trim.

Martian Marauder

Fold a sheet of notebook or typing paper in half the short way; then unfold it and place it with the long side near you, as seen in Illus. 137.

Illus. 137

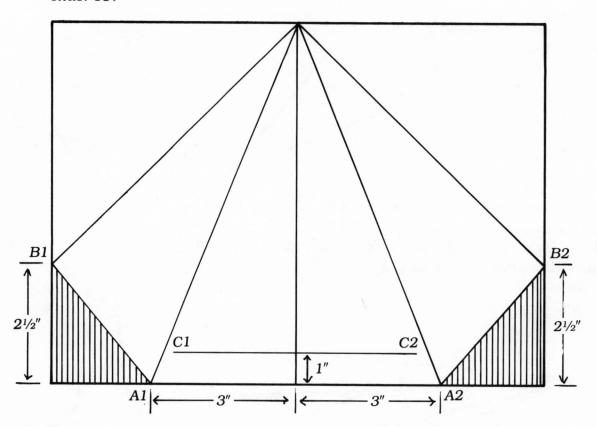

Locate points A1 and A2 3 inches to the left and to the right of the middle. Mark them and connect them with the nose point so that they match Illus. 137.

Measure up 2½ inches along the right and left sides of the paper. These are points B1 and B2. Mark these points, and join them with the nose.

Draw a line connecting A1 and B1; then draw another one connecting A2 and B2. Measure up 1 inch from the bottom of the paper for points C1 and C2. Mark these points. Cut out the darkened areas in Illus. 137.

Turn the paper over, and fold along lines A1 and B1, as well as A2 and B2. The edges of the folded sides may overlap just a bit, but this is fine. Martian Marauder should now look like Illus. 138. Refold the paper down the middle so that it looks like Illus. 139.

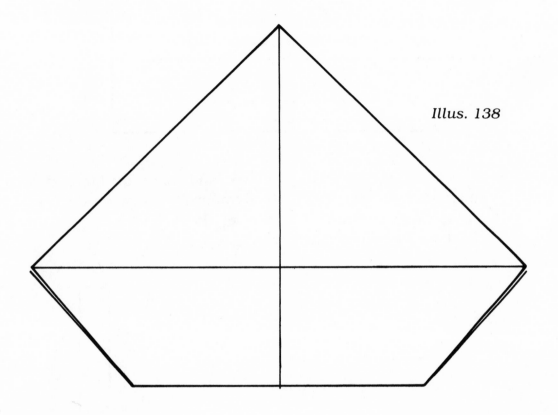

Illus. 138

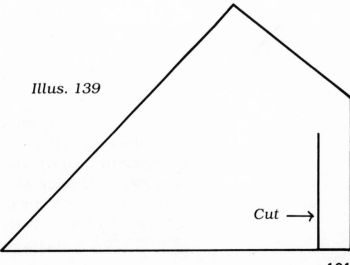

Illus. 139

Cut along line C, as you see in Illus. 139.

After making this cut, push up at the arrow in Illus. 139. This will turn the aircraft's tail inside out so that it looks like Illus. 140.

Cut ⟶

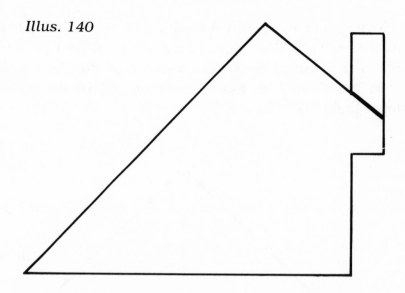

Illus. 140

Now fold both wings down and Martian Marauder matches Illus. 141. Use a bit of transparent tape on the vertical stabilizer (that's the part of the tail sticking up) to hold the two sides together.

Illus. 141

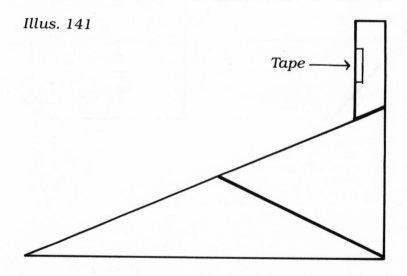

Tape ⟶

Pull the wings up so that they stick straight out from the fuselage; then lift them about ¼ inch. A little strip of transparent tape will hold them in place. Launch your Martian Marauder. Play with the trim to get a good flight. You may have to place one or two paper clips on the fuselage to get the best trim or move them back a little way from the nose for proper flight.

Transporter

The Transporter requires three sheets of notebook or typing paper. Place one sheet directly on top of the second. Fold both sheets in half the long way to make the central fold. Unfold them and place them in front of you to match Illus. 142.

Measure 1 inch to the right and the left of the middle along the bottom of the paper. These are points A1 and A2.

Measure ½ inch to the right and the left of the middle at the top of the paper. Mark these points and connect them with A1 and A2 with straight lines. Check Illus. 142 to be sure your lines match those in the drawing.

Now measure up 4 inches from the bottom along the outer edges of the paper. These are points B1 and B2.

Measure 1 inch to the right and left of the middle at the nose. Connect these points with B1 and B2. Illus. 142 shows these lines.

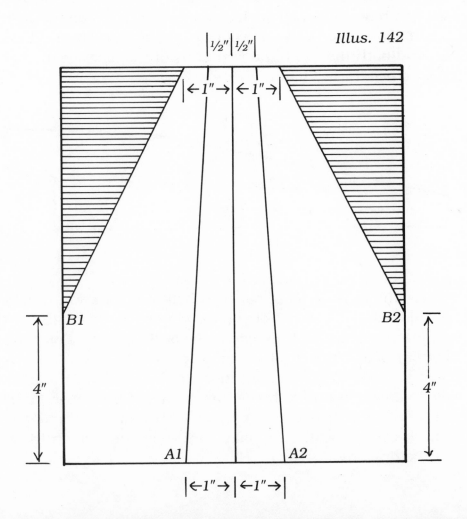

Illus. 142

Cut off and discard the darkened areas in Illus. 142. Remember to hold both pieces of paper firmly together as you cut. Refold the paper along the central fold, so that it looks like Illus. 143.

Illus. 143

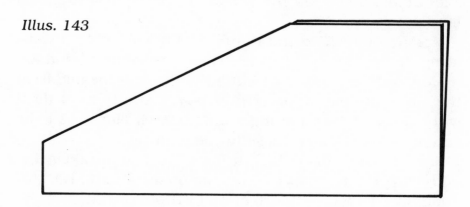

Fold both wings down along line A1 and A2; then lift the wings up so that they stick straight out from the fuselage as in Illus. 144. Wrap a short piece of transparent tape around both the front and rear ends of the fuselage to hold it together during flight.

Illus. 144

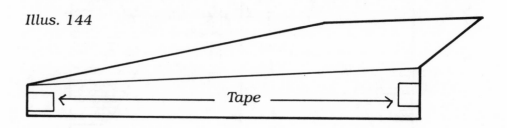

Tape

Set this part of Transporter to one side.

Fold the third sheet of paper in half the short way, unfold it, and place it in front of you as you see in Illus. 145.

Measure 2 inches from each side of the middle along the bottom of the paper. Mark these points A1 and A2 as in Illus. 145. In the same way, measure 1 inch from the middle to the right and to the left at the top of the paper. Mark these points; then connect them with points A1 and A2. Check with Illus. 145 to make sure your lines match those in the drawing.

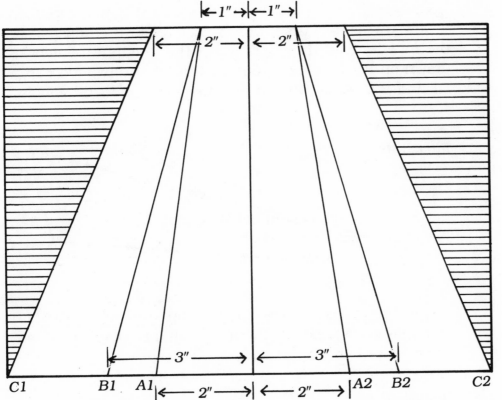

Next, measure 3 inches from the middle along the bottom of the paper to the right and the left. These points are B1 and B2. Draw straight lines between B1 and B2 and the points at the top of the paper. Check Illus. 145 before you draw these lines just to make sure you are on the right track.

There is only one more pair of lines left. Mark the bottom corners of the paper points C1 and C2; then measure 2 inches to the right and 2 inches to the left of the middle on the top of the paper. Join those points with C1 and C2, as in Illus. 145. Remove the darkened areas in Illus. 145 by just cutting along the lines from C1 and C2.

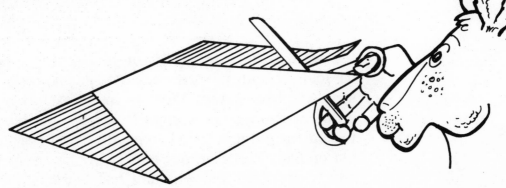

Now it's folding time, but do not refold the paper along the middle. Fold the paper along the four lines which are drawn on it—two lines from A1 and A2 and two more from B1 and B2. Illus. 146 shows Transporter after these folds.

Illus. 146

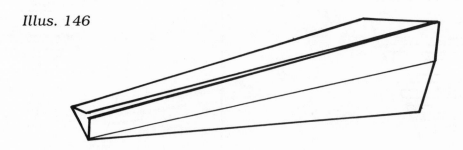

Use three pieces of transparent tape to hold this part of Transporter together in its proper shape. Illus. 147 shows where to put the tape.

Illus. 147

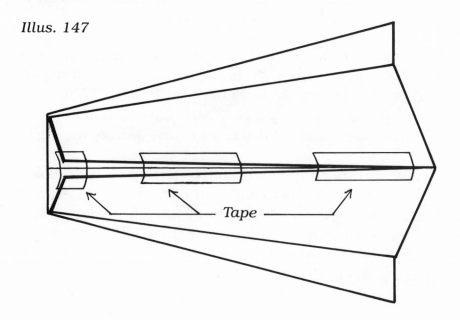

Place this part on top of the first part. Be sure the middle folds of both parts line up. Attach the sections with five strips of transparent tape as in Illus. 148. Fold the two strips at the rear of the craft over the bottom layer of the top part; then fold them under the lower part of the Transporter. Place three or four paper clips on Transporter's nose and you're ready for your first test flight.

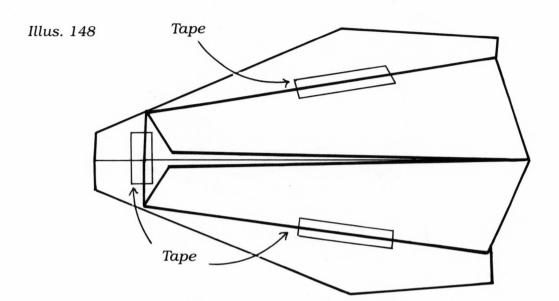

Tape

Tape

Transporter can be launched fairly hard since its double layer of material on the lower section makes it more solid than many paper airplanes.

If you want to do a little research, make another Transporter with only one layer of paper for the bottom half of the craft. You probably will also have some design ideas of your own, so why not sit down and make some fliers from your own designs? Don't worry if a design idea does not fly—just change the design and try again. That's what designing is all about. It gives you a chance to try your own ideas.

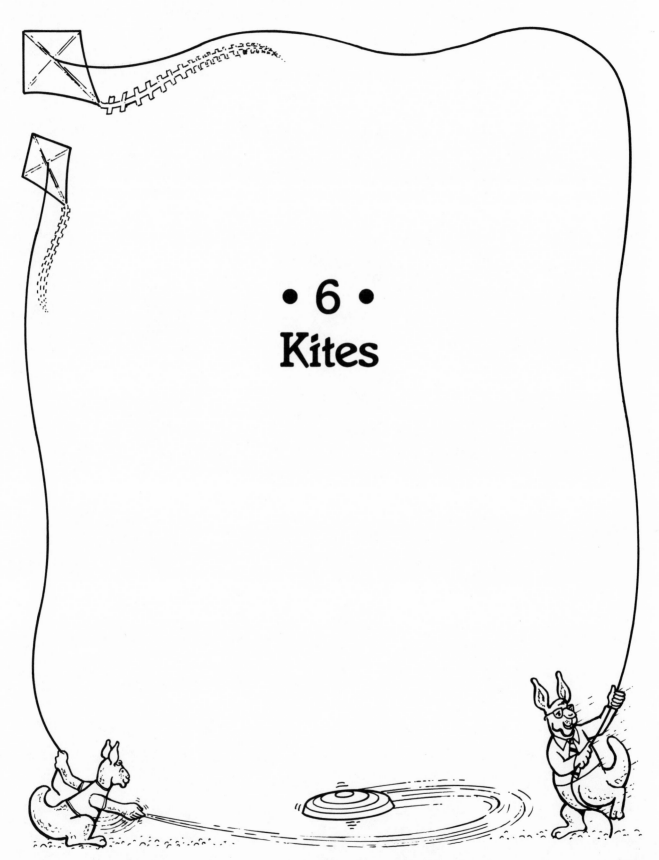

• 6 •
Kites

Flying kites is a lot different from flying other paper toys. For one thing, except for very simple kites, it takes a little more time and effort to build a kite. For another thing, kites have to be flown outside in a strong breeze.

Kites may be simple, or as complicated as the huge Chinese dragon kites which require several people and many control strings for flying.

Sometimes the trees have the control!

Tiny

A sheet of notebook paper or typing paper can easily be turned into this simple kite.

Begin by making the paper square (if you forgot how, just go back to page 36). Fold the square diagonally in half so that it matches Illus. 149; then fold the bottom edge of the top layer of paper up so that it is even with the middle fold. This is the dotted line in Illus. 149. Crease the fold, turn the paper over, and fold the other side up in the same way. At this point Tiny looks like Illus. 150.

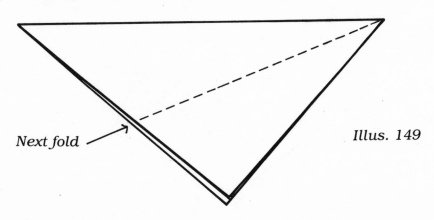

Next fold

Illus. 149

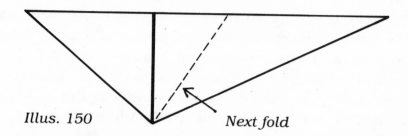

Illus. 150   Next fold

The dotted line in Illus. 150 shows the next fold. Make this fold and crease well. Turn Tiny over and fold the other side the same way. Illus. 151 now shows your kite. It also shows you where to place a piece of transparent tape. This tape overlaps the fold you just made. Attach this strip of tape to both of Tiny's wings (at least they look like wings).

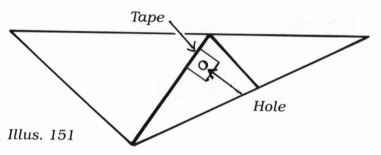

Tape

Hole

Illus. 151

Illus. 151 also shows where to make a hole. Carefully poke this hole through the two layers of paper and tape. It needs to be only about ⅛ inch across, but it must go through the middle of the tape. Make a hole in each wing.

Now get a piece of thread about 1 foot long of any color you like. Push one end of the thread through the hole in the wing nearest you and tie it firmly; then do the same with the other end of the thread on the other wing. Tiny looks like Illus. 152 by now.

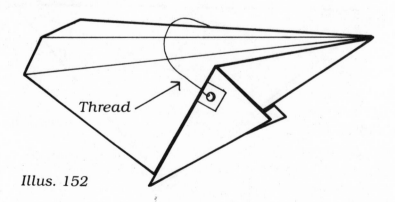

Thread

Illus. 152

This thread is called a bridle. It helps direct the kite while it is flying.

Tiny needs a tail. Cut three strips of notebook paper about 1 × 11 inches. Tape or staple them into a tail about 3 feet long. Fasten one end of the tail to Tiny's rear point with tape or a staple. It should now look like Illus. 153.

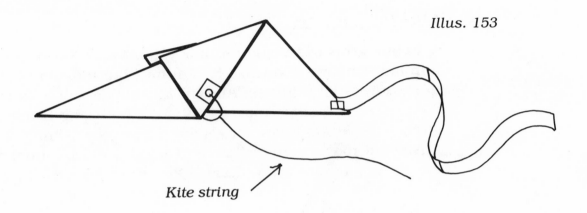

Illus. 153

Kite string

Tie your kite string to the bridle and start looking for a strong breeze.

Before looking for that breeze, there are a few things we need to cover about kite flying.

The length of a kite's tail keeps the kite steady in the air, not the weight. So a kite's tail doesn't need to be heavy. The harder the wind blows, the longer the tail should be.

The best wind for kite flying is a steady breeze strong enough to bend small branches. A really strong wind may damage your kite before you get it into the air. A strong wind can also collapse your kite or break the string, once in the air.

Kite string needs to be strong and very lightweight, so the best thing to use is nylon. Sewing thread is good for Tiny, unless your mother objects. Better check.

To launch Tiny, stand with your back to the breeze. Let out a bit of string and the wind should take Tiny into the air. No matter what you've seen, you don't need to run to launch a kite. If the wind is strong enough, a kite will lift off and climb as you let out string.

You might think that Tiny wouldn't need much wind, but in fact it needs more wind than do some of the larger kites. This is because it has such a small amount of surface in relation to its weight.

If Tiny tears or loses its tail, don't worry about it—it only takes a couple of minutes to build a new one. If it's only a tear, a piece of tape should do the job.

Old-Fashioned

To build this Old-Fashioned kite you must first construct a frame. Tiny was too small for a frame, but most kites require frames for stiffness. Ancient kite builders used bamboo strips, but since most of us don't have any bamboo strips lying around, dowel rods are the next-best thing.

A dowel rod is a round piece of wood, available from a lumberyard or hardware dealer. Dowels are usually 3 feet long, which is just fine for kite building. Select dowels which are either ⅛ inch or ³⁄₁₆ inch in diameter. These will make your kite stiff without being too heavy.

Dowels cost about 20 cents each (better buy a few because your next project will need them, too).

You'll also need a covering for your kite that is both light in weight and strong enough not to tear easily. Try not to use newspaper unless you can't find anything better. Of course, when a rip does occur, you can usually patch it with a strip of transparent tape.

I don't think that's what they meant!

Gift-wrapping paper makes a good kite if it's thin enough. Never, *never* use wrapping paper with foil on it.

Another good idea is plastic trash bags. They are tough and fairly light, and as long as they are not the heavy-duty kind, they'll make a great kite covering or skin. Cut one half off a large-size bag and you're all set.

Now for the building. Cut one dowel rod 30 inches long and another 24 inches in length. To make these cuts, take a knife and *carefully* roll the dowel under it a bit. (If you have a cutting board handy, place it under the dowel.) When you have made a small cut, snap off the end of the rod.

Place the two dowel rods as you see them in Illus. 154. Put the shorter rod about 10 inches from the top of the longer rod. For now, use a strip of tape to hold them together. Wrap the tape around the crossing of the dowels, and make sure it crosses them diagonally in both directions.

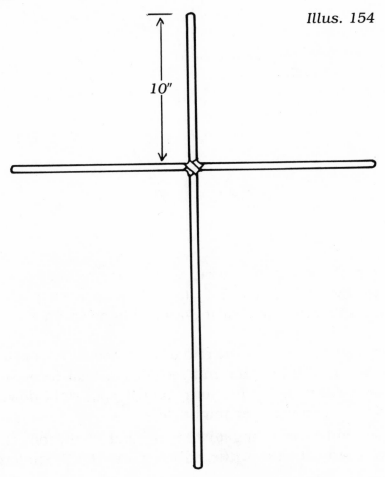

Illus. 154

10"

After wrapping the tape around the rods take a piece of string and wrap it over the tape. Tie it tightly so that the rods don't slip.

Now comes the hard part. Tie a border of string all the way around the kite, as in Illus. 155.

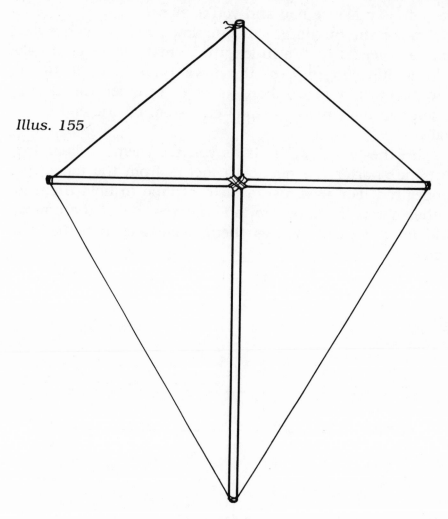

Illus. 155

Begin at the top, and wrap the string around the end of the rod several times. Tie it, and wrap a strip of tape around the string so that it doesn't slip down on the dowel rod.

Don't try to cut into the end of your dowel. This is a very complicated thing to do and requires special tools, and if you try to use your knife, your rod will split right down the middle, and your finger might, too.

After tying the string to the top end of the dowel rod, move on to the end of the dowel at the right. Stretch the string tight, wrap it around the tip of the rod three times and tape it into place.

Move to the bottom dowel rod end and repeat the process; then go on to the left-hand rod and finally end up at the top. Always wind the string around the dowel three times and wrap a strip of tape around it. Tie the string off at the top and your kite frame is finished.

When you're doing all this tying and taping, don't be afraid to ask for help. It never hurts to have an extra pair of hands to hold things together, and it's better to wait for help than to try it alone and end up frustrated.

Lay the frame down flat on the skin material. Trim the edges so that the material is about 1 inch larger than the frame all the way around. Illus. 156 shows how it should look.

Illus. 156

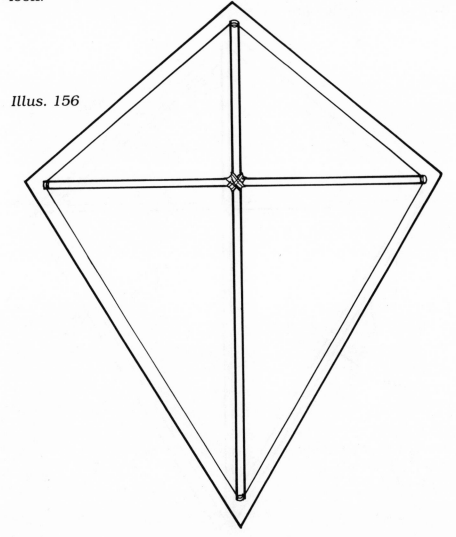

Cut out a piece of material at each corner in the shape of a V. This will keep the skin from bunching up. Illus. 157 shows how this should look.

Cut "U" shape

Illus. 157

Fold the edge of the cover over the string between two dowel rods and fasten it down with strips of tape. Be sure to keep the covering tight and avoid wrinkles. (Here you may need that extra pair of hands again.)

Move diagonally across the kite to fold and tape the next edge into place. Illus. 158 shows the kite now. Do the other two edges in the same way.

Illus. 158

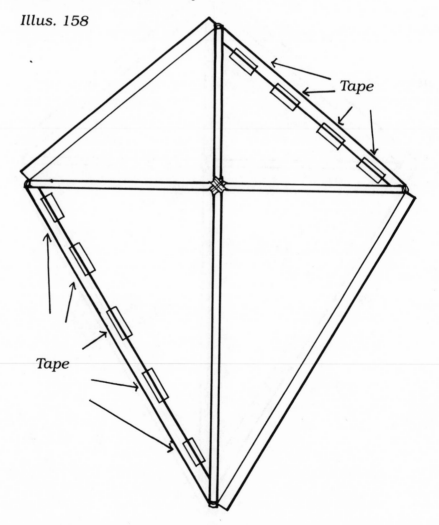

Tape

Tape

I thought flying them was hard!

Fasten the dowel rods against the cover with tape. Illus.
159 shows how to place the tape.

Illus. 159

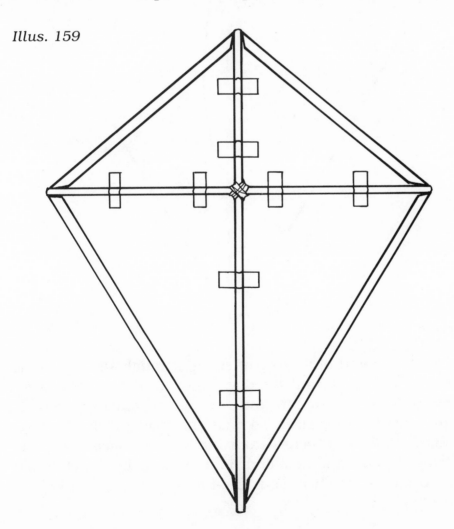

Now you need to make the bridle holes (the holes that hold the bridle). Place strips of tape as you see them in Illus. 160. These will keep the bridle holes from tearing as the kite flies. Put one strip 3 inches from the top of the kite, and the other 8 inches from the bottom. Poke the holes through the tape and the skin.

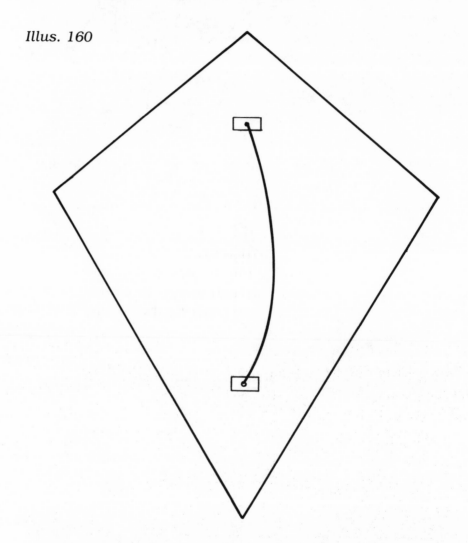

Illus. 160

Push the end of a piece of string through the top bridle hole and tie it around the dowel rod. Run the string along the cover side of the kite and down to the other bridle hole, but leave enough slack so that the bridle string can be pulled up 6 or 8 inches from the kite's surface. Push the string through the hole and tie it around the dowel. When the bridle is attached, your Old-Fashioned kite should look like Illus. 160.

Tie the kite string securely to the bridle about ⅓ of the way down from the top.

Now turn the kite over so that you can bow it. Take a piece of string and make a small loop in it. Slip the loop over one end of the short dowel rod and pull it right down against the loop already there.

Pull the other end of this string across to the other end of the dowel rod, but before you tie it down, push down on the middle of the dowel rod and gently put a bend, or bow, in it. When it is about 4 inches from the string to the middle of the dowel rod, the bow is just right. Wrap the end of the string tightly around the end of the dowel rod and tie it firmly to keep the bow. Illus. 161 shows it in place.

Illus. 161

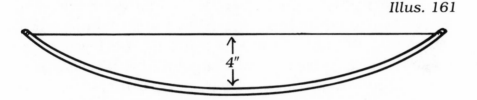

Make the tail out of narrow cloth strips, about 6 feet long. After a few flights, you can make it longer if you want. Illus. 162 shows the tail in place. Tie a piece of string to the end of the tail; then attach the strips to it.

Illus. 162

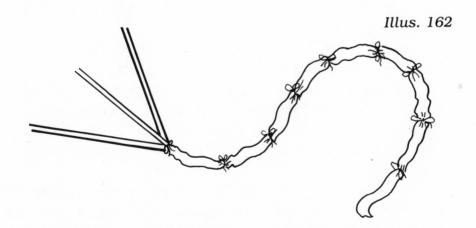

You can also make a tail out of 6 pieces of notebook paper. Roll them up; then tie them in the middle. Move the string up, and tie it around again. Keep doing this until you reach the end; then tie it to the dowel.

You're now ready to fly.

With the breeze or wind at your back, let out 10 to 12 feet of string. Hold the kite up or, better yet, have someone else hold it. As soon as the wind catches it, let go. Old-Fashioned doesn't need a toss or throw. If the wind is strong enough, the kite will rise on its own.

If your kite slips back to the ground, it is probably because there is not enough wind. Be sure you have the wind at your back and try again. It does not take a lot of wind to get a kite up, but it does take a fairly steady breeze, so you may have to wait for it.

Sometimes there may be plenty of wind and a kite won't go into the air, and if it does, it doesn't seem sure it wants to fly. When this happens, try shortening the bridle string a bit. Your kite must "stand up" in the air in order to fly properly. If the top of the kite leans too far towards you, make the bridle string a little longer (but don't make it too long or the kite will fall backwards). Sometimes the proper bridle length is a matter of trial and error.

If your kite goes up a little way, then comes down in a dive, then tries to turn up, it is because the tail is too short. Add another strip of cloth to the tail and see if that does not take care of things.

Now that you've gotten flying down, here are a few things to remember. Don't fly a kite when it is raining or there is a chance of lightning. Ben Franklin was very lucky he did not end up with a bad case of electrocution.

Keep your kite away from power lines and trees. Both of them do terrible things to kites and kite fliers.

If you want to build a new kite, salvage the dowel rods. You can use these rods again and again, unless they break.

Illus. 163

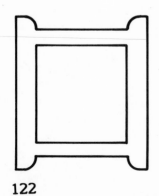

You can wind your string onto a hollow cardboard tube, or you can make a string reel such as the one pictured in Illus. 163.

Draw a pattern for the reel with the hole large enough to slip your hand into (if you make it about 4 inches across the middle, it should be about the right size); then trace the pattern onto some cardboard. Make four or five layers and glue them together. Tie one end of the kite string to the reel; then wind it onto the reel and you're done.

Hex

This kite is a bit more difficult to build because Hex (which stands for hexagonal) uses three dowel rods in its frame.

For Hex's frame you need two 36-inch rods and one 24-inch rod. Assemble them as shown in Illus. 164 with the short rod crossing the longer rods in the middle. Use a strip of tape to hold the rods together; then lightly wrap and tie a piece of string around them.

Illus. 164

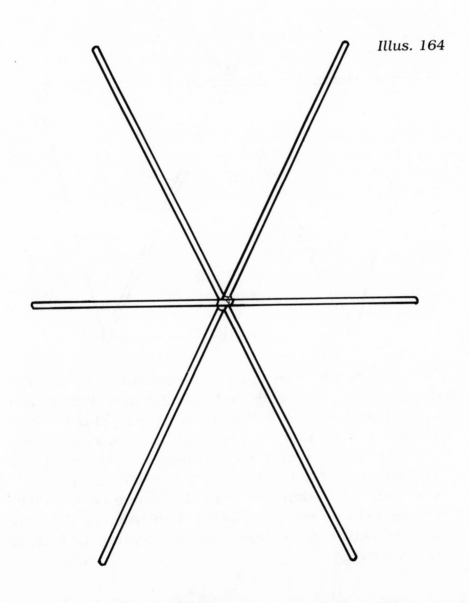

Next, tie a string to the end of the dowel rod shown by the arrow in Illus. 165. Use a bit of tape to hold it in place.

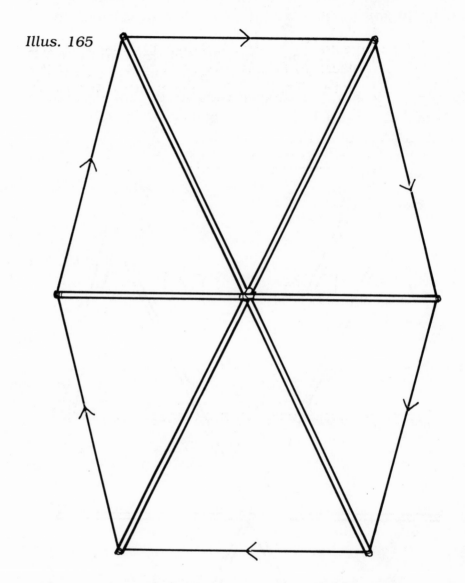

Illus. 165

Slowly work your way around the outside of the dowels, wrapping the string tightly and taping it into place at each end until you are back to the starting point. This is where a helper could be much appreciated. It is difficult to keep all the rods together while you're wrapping and taping. If it gets a little out of line, don't worry. Hex will still fly.

Cut your kite's skin and place the frame on top of it. Trim the skin so that it is about 1 inch larger than the frame, and cut out the little V-shaped areas at the ends of the dowel rods.

When you begin to fold and tape the skin to the strings, remember to do the area between two dowel rods; then do the area directly *opposite* that section, so that you stretch the skin as tight as you can.

Tape the frame to the cover as shown in Illus. 166. You also see three places to attach a layer of tape to the cover for the bridle holes. That's right—there are three bridle holes in Hex.

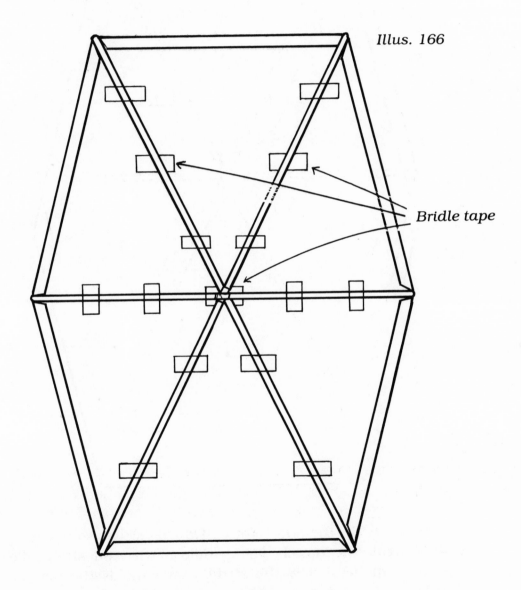

Illus. 166

Bridle tape

Remember to press this tape onto the cover only. It does not go over the frame. It is also a good idea to put tape on both sides of the cover at these places for added strength.

Illus. 167 shows the bridle strings in place. The top string should be 9 inches down from the upper ends of the two dowel rods. Tie one end of the lower bridle string to the upper string, and the other end to where the three dowel rods meet.

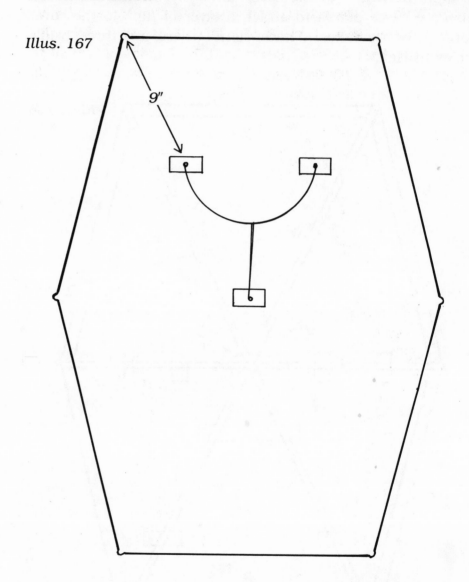

Illus. 167

9"

Put a bow in the short dowel. Do this slowly so that you don't break the dowel. The middle of the rod should be about 4 inches below the string which holds the bow in place.

Attach the tail by tying a short piece of string to the lower ends of the two dowel rods. You can see this in Illus. 167.

Tie one end of the kite string firmly to the bridle strings and Hex is ready to fly.

Once you get into kite flying, try to design your own kite. Just use the ideas you learned here and try your hand at a different design. Round kites will fly but are hard to build. Rectangular kites usually do a good job of flying and are easier. Think about a triangular kite or one with five sides. You could even try changing Hex a bit by setting the cross-piece higher. Just remember to take your time when building your kites and always fly them safely.

Don't let Hex put the hex on you!

Index